How to Use

 **All you need:**

A pencil, pencil sharpener and an eraser.

 **Start drawing:**

The left layout shows you exactly how to draw the object step by step.

Use the right layout to follow along the drawing, soon you will finish the object in few steps.

Some erasing maybe necessary along the steps.

 **Coloring:**

When you are finished, you can also add more details and colour it.

Instructions

1

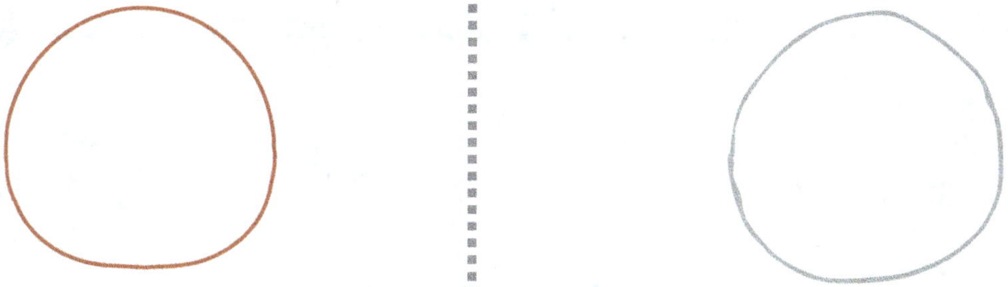

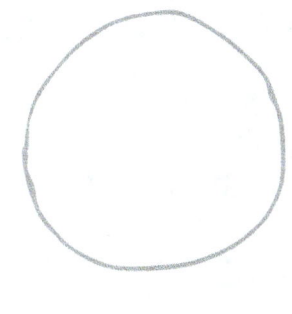

2

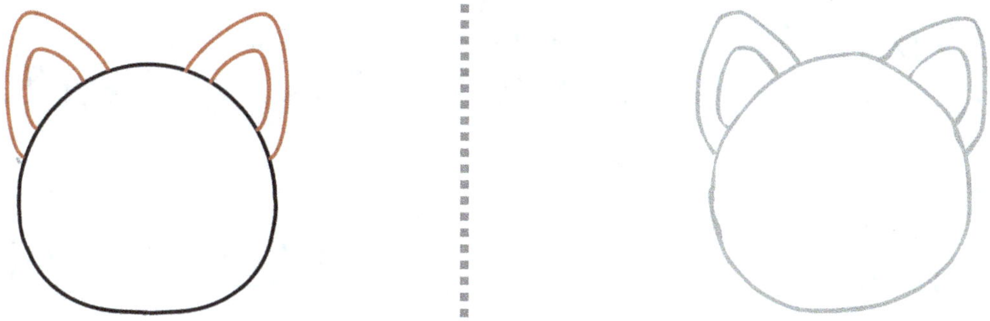

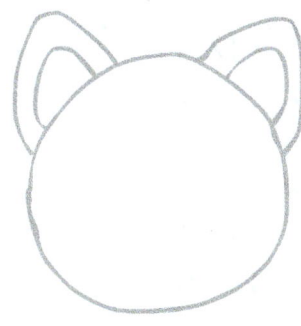

3

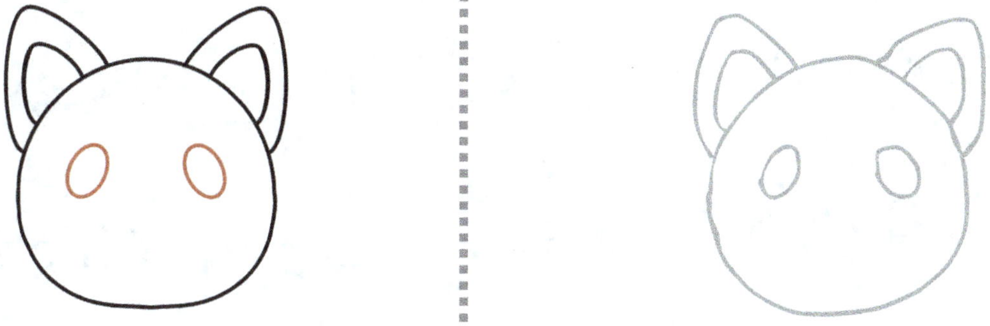

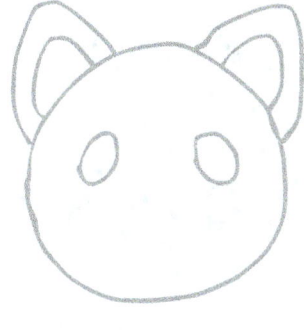

4

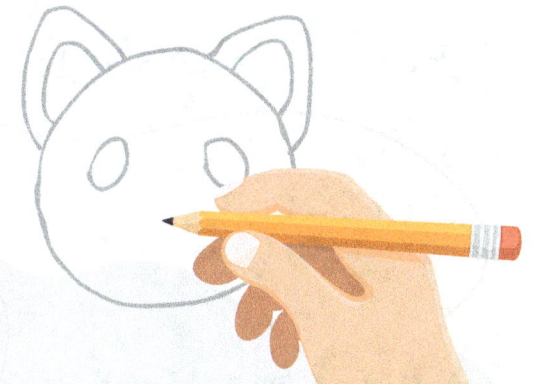

Check List

The following directed drawings are included:

1. ☐ Kitty/ Cat
2. ☐ Puppy/ Dog
3. ☐ Bunny
4. ☐ Lion
5. ☐ Tiger
6. ☐ Zebra
7. ☐ Gorilla
8. ☐ Snake
9. ☐ Elephant
10. ☐ Giraffe

11. ☐ Clown Fish
12. ☐ Dolphin
13. ☐ Sea Turtle
14. ☐ Octopus
15. ☐ Cow
16. ☐ Piggy
17. ☐ Chicken
18. ☐ Sheep
19. ☐ Horse
20 ☐ Kangaroo

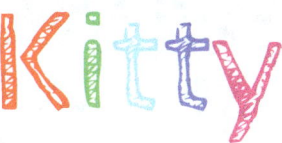

Kitty

1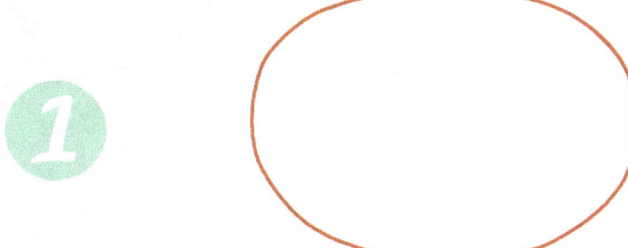

2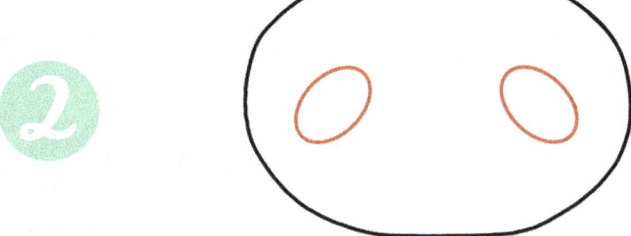

3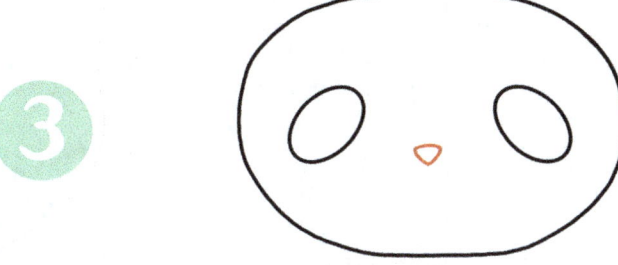

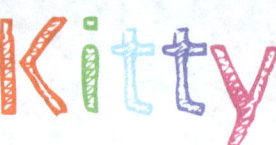

4

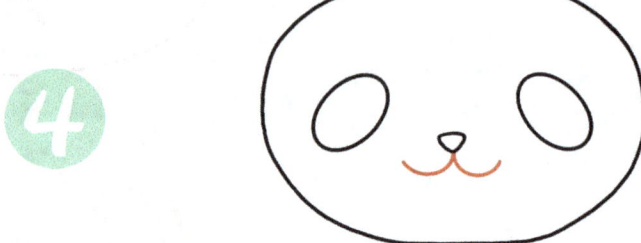

5

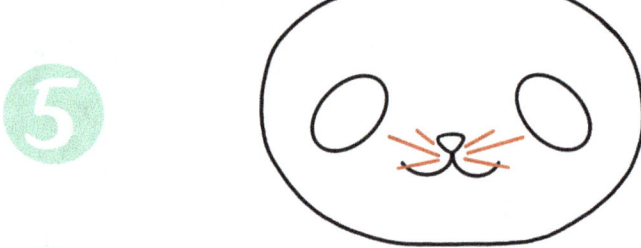

6

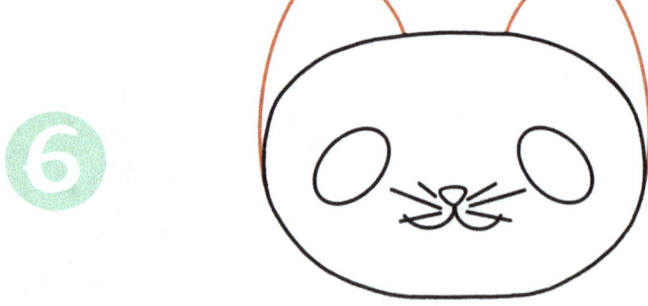

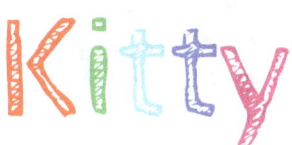

7

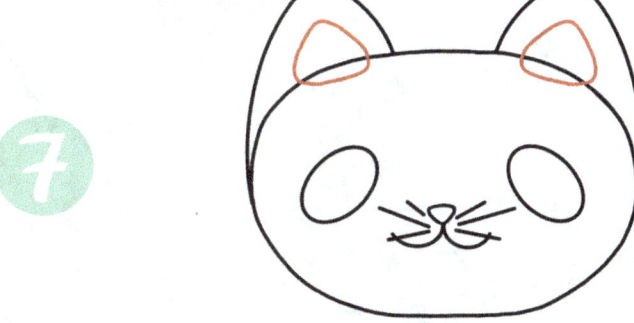

8

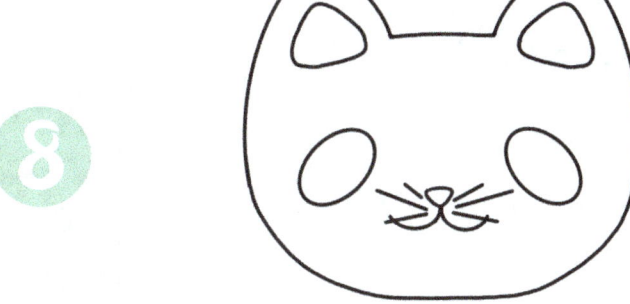

9

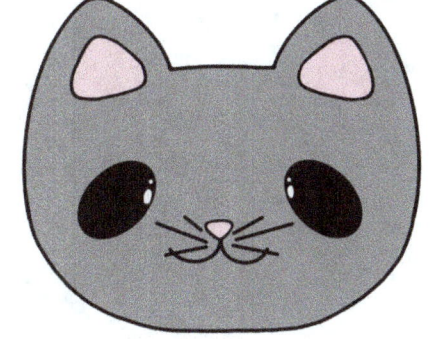

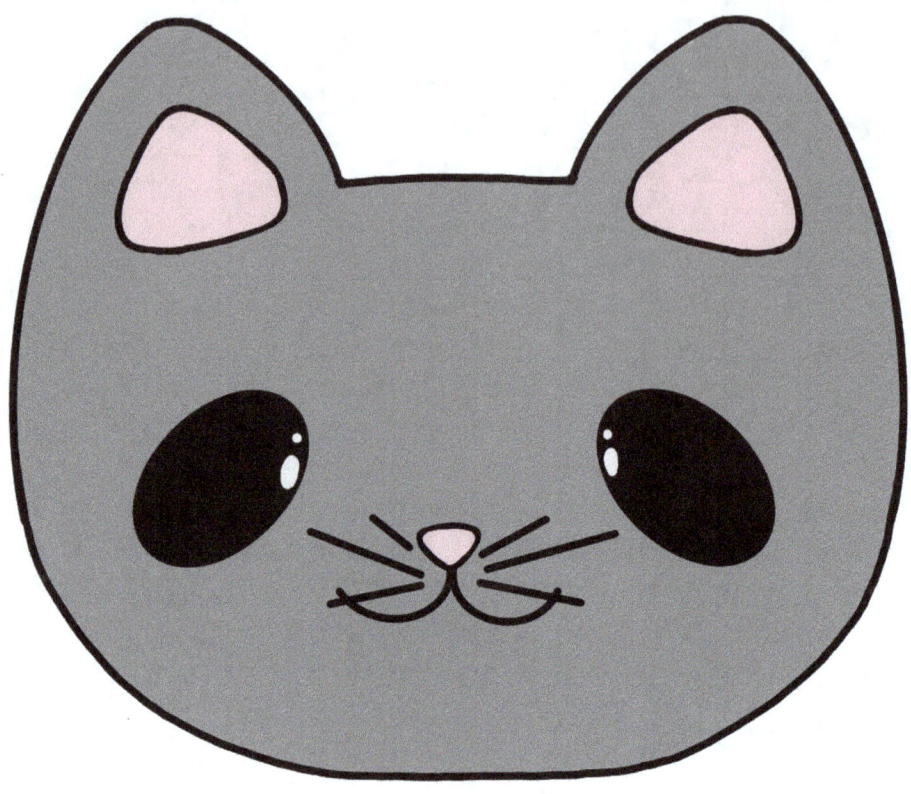

Puppy

1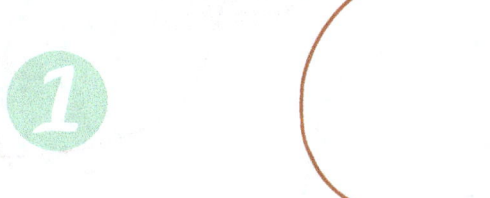

2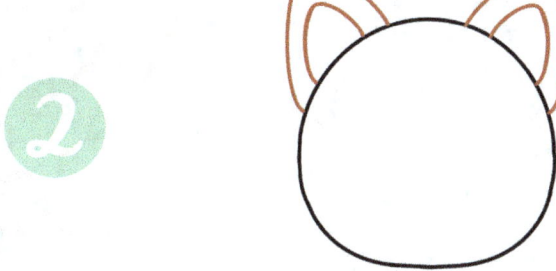

3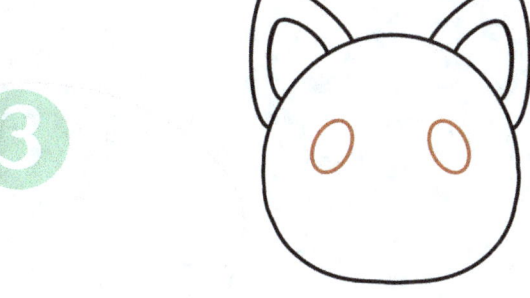

4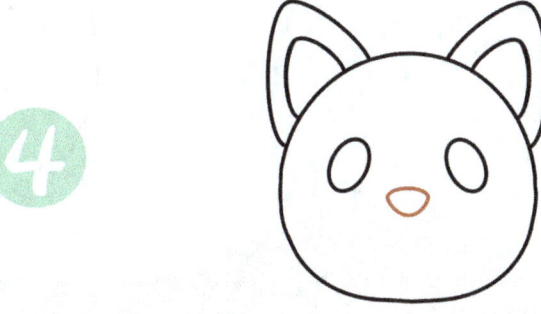

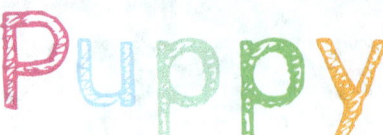

5

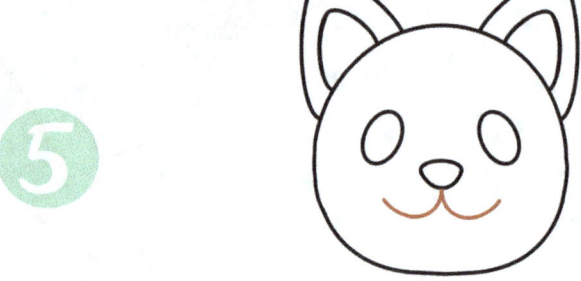

6

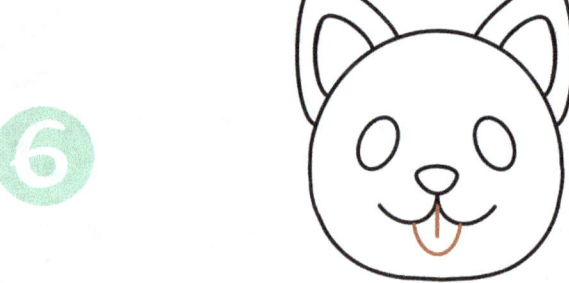

7

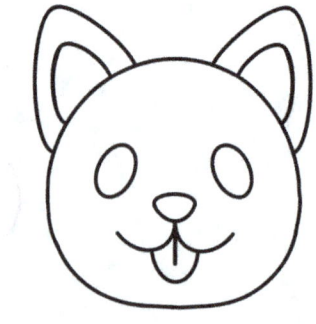

8

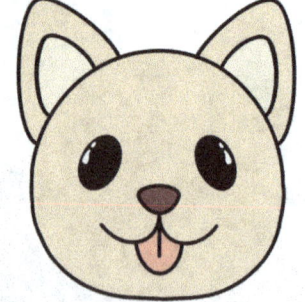

Puppy

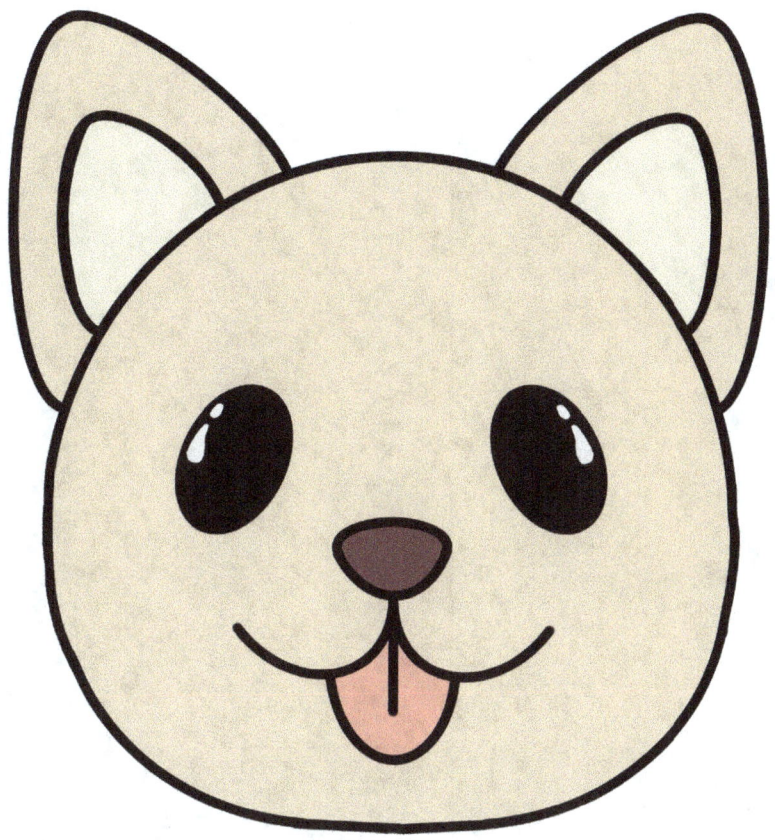

Bunny

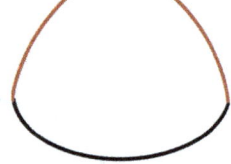

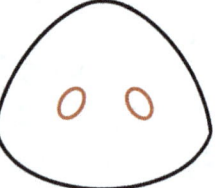

Bunny

 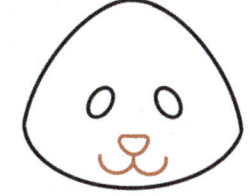

 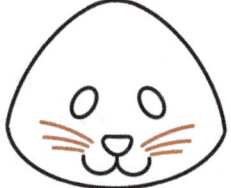

 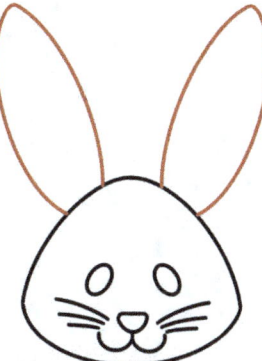

Bunny

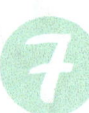

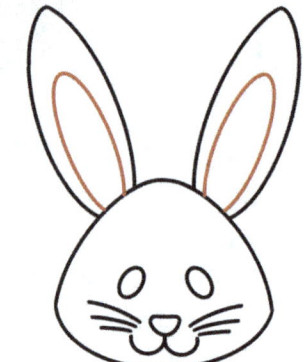

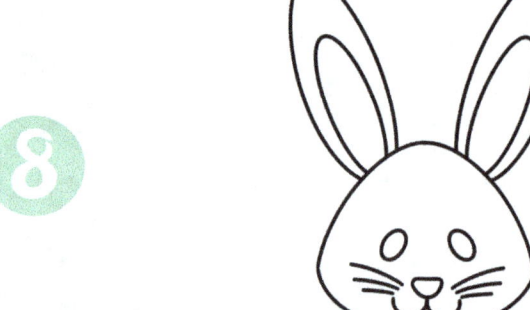

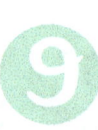

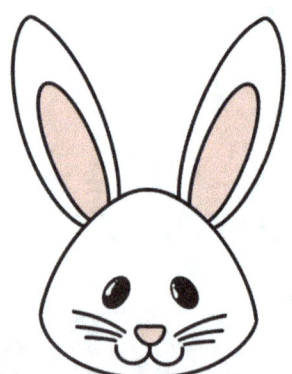

Bunny

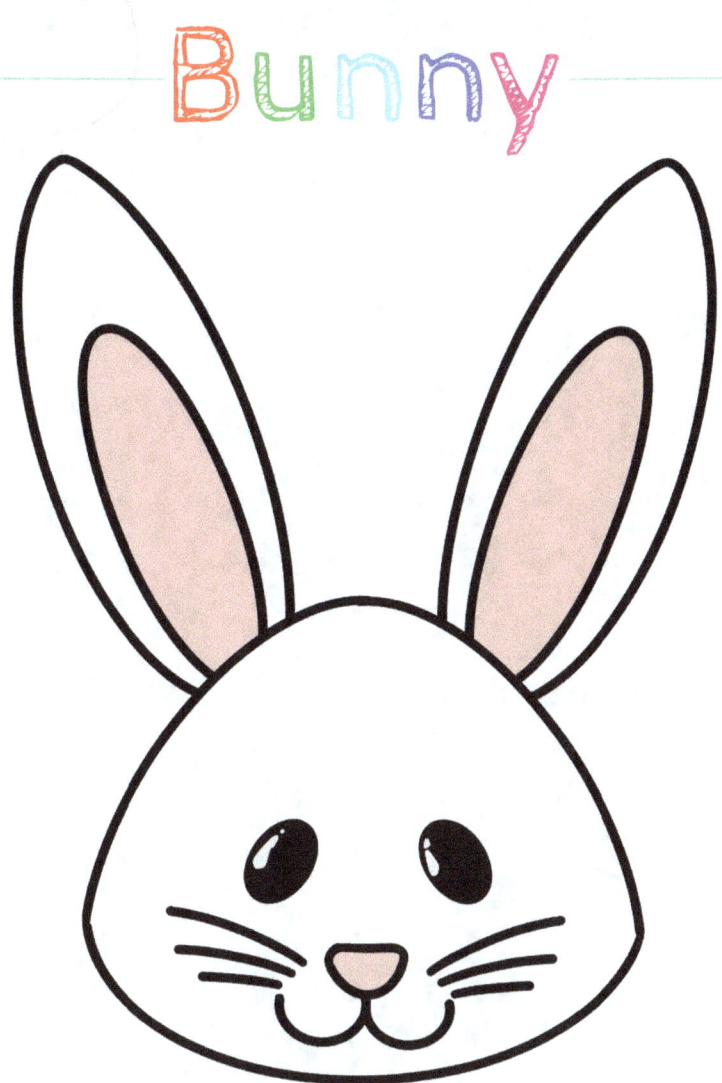

Lion

1

2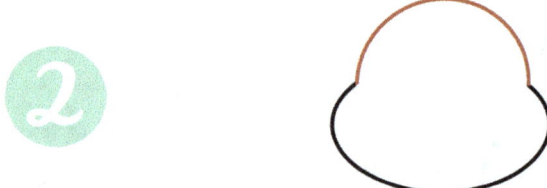

3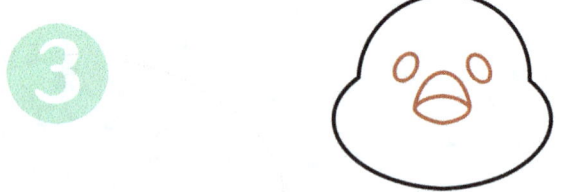

4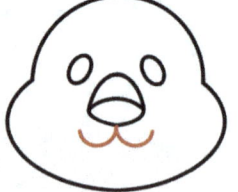

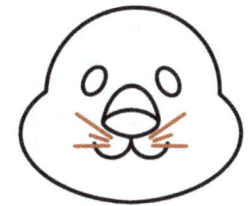

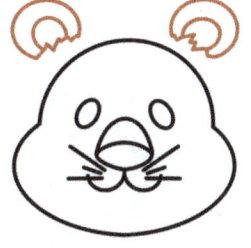

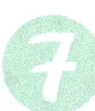

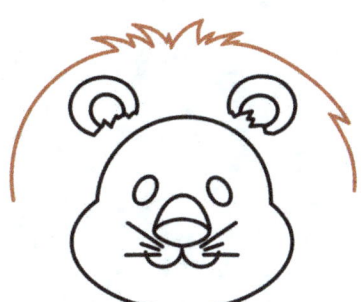

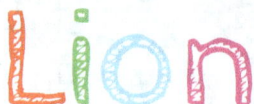

Lion

 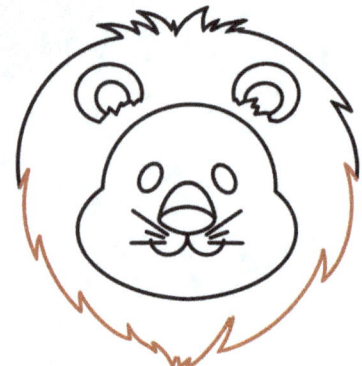

 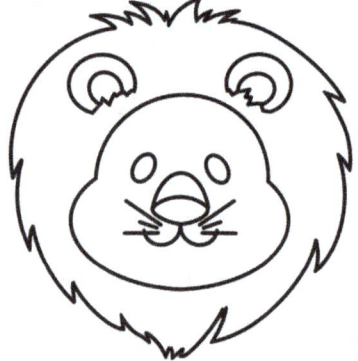

 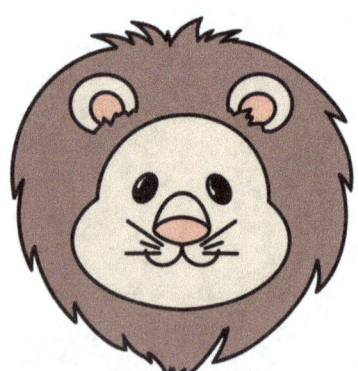

Lion

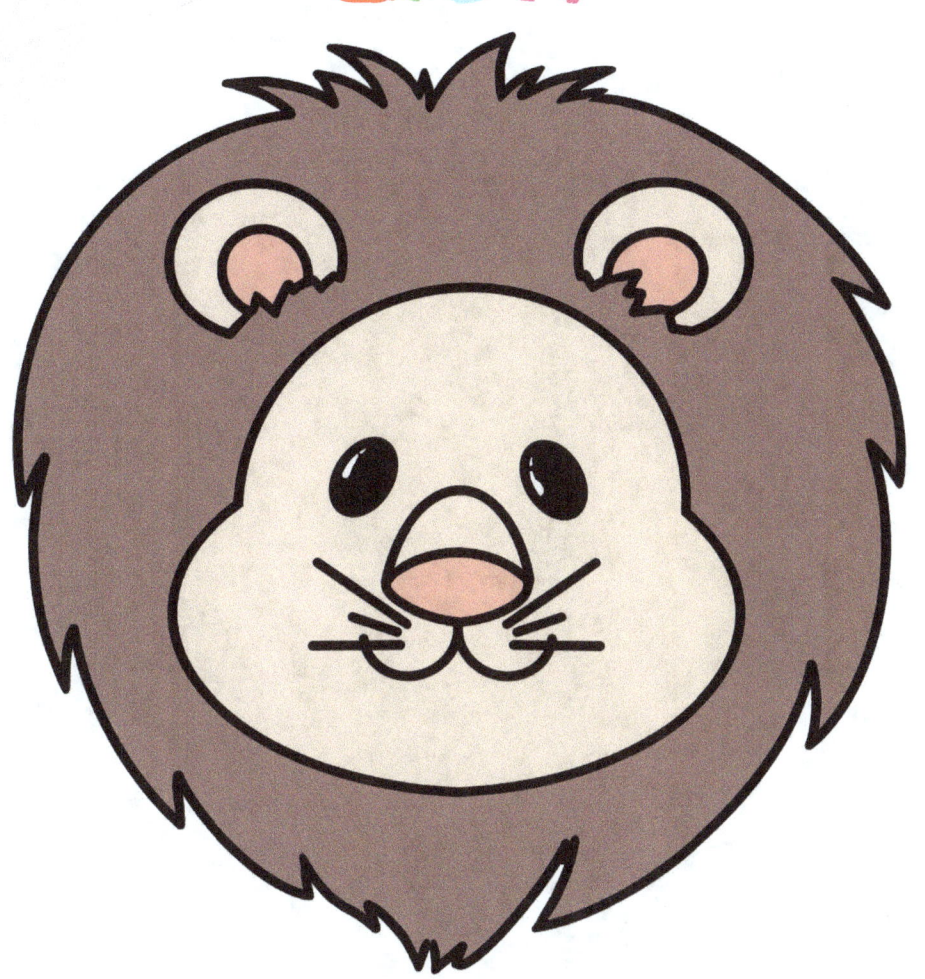

Tiger

1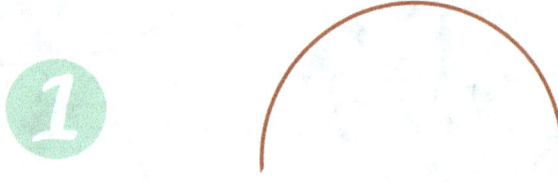

2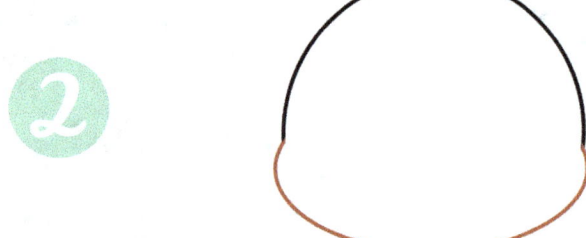

3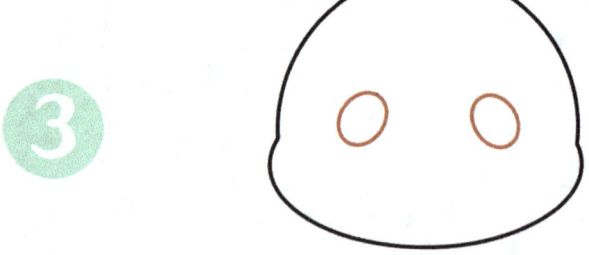

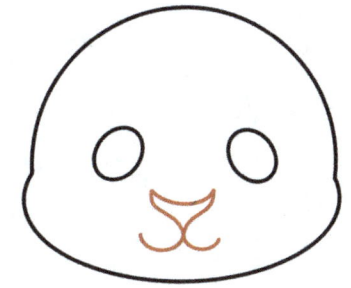

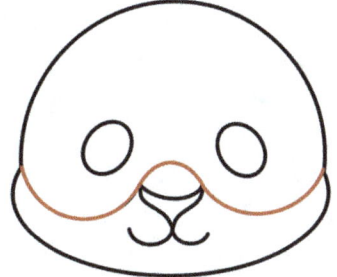

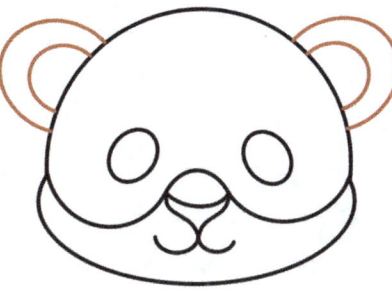

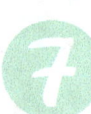 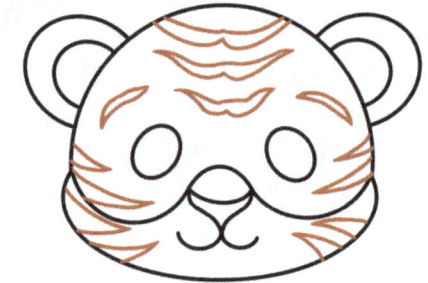

 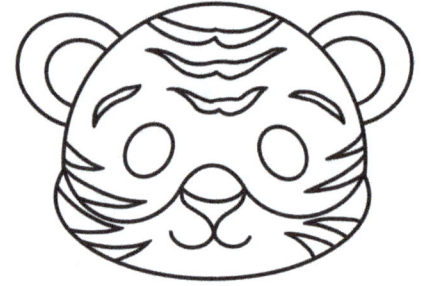

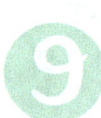 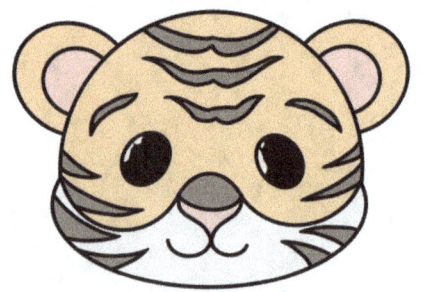

Tiger

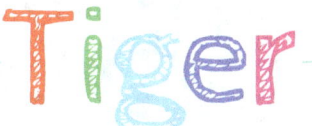

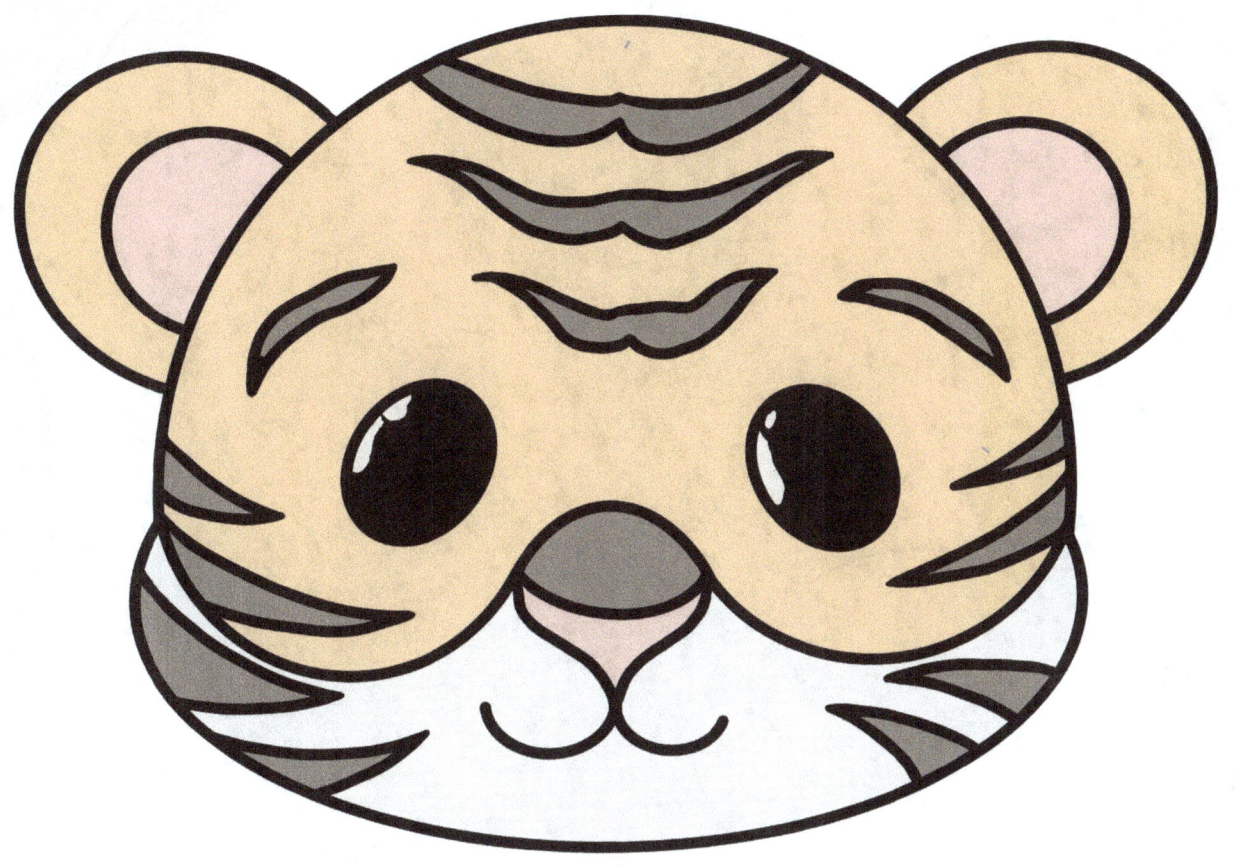

Zebra

 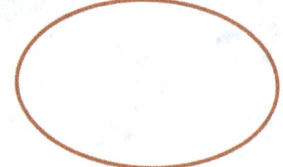

 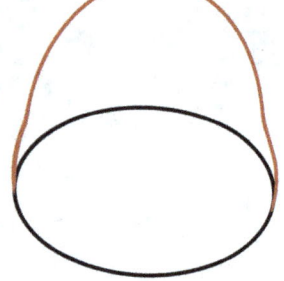

 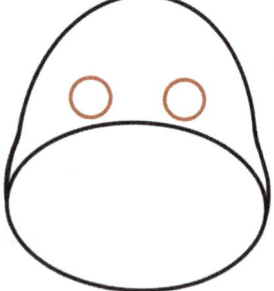

 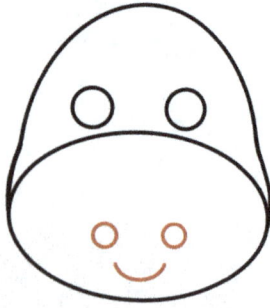

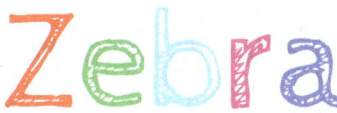

5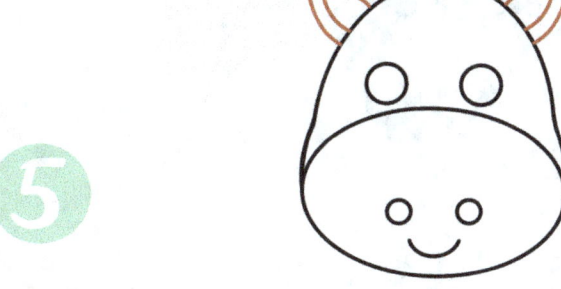

6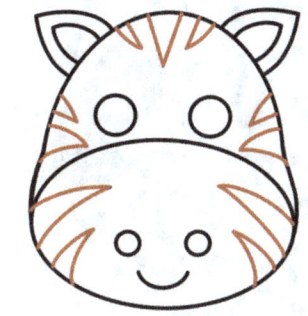

7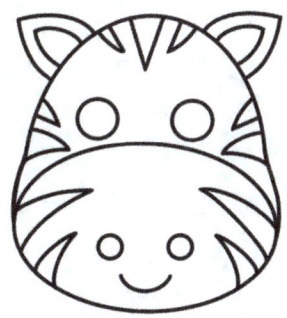

8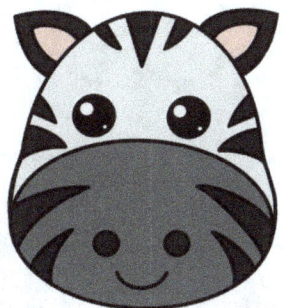

Zebra

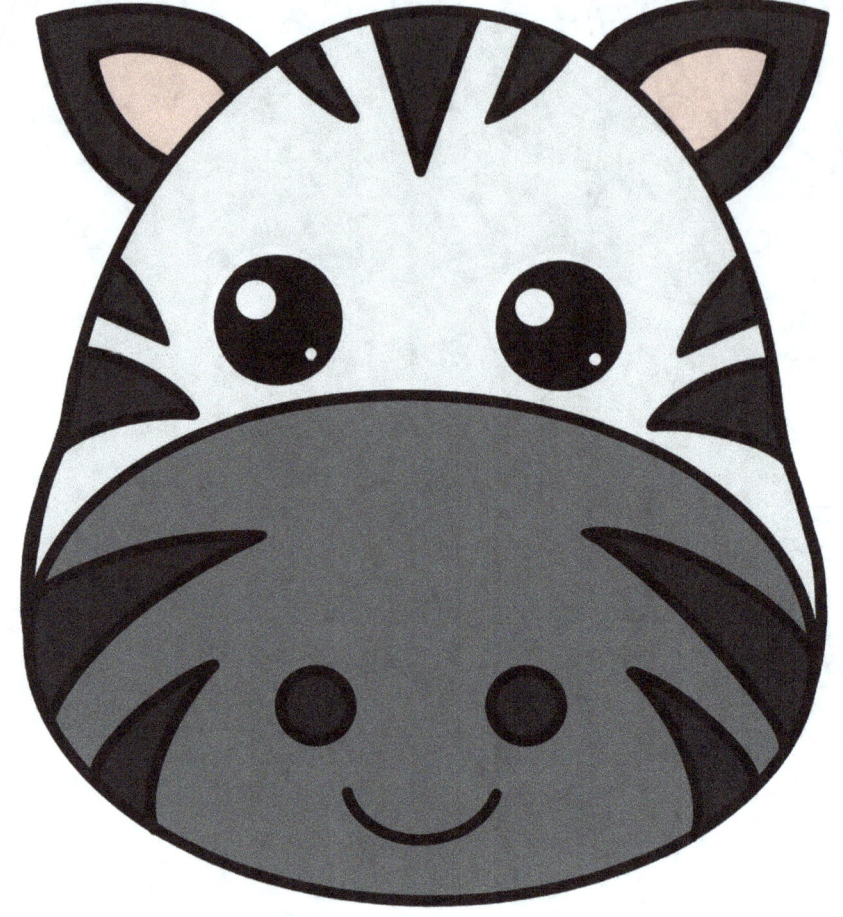

Gorilla

1

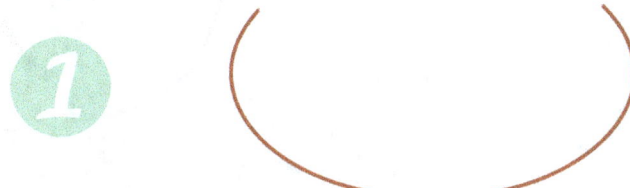

2

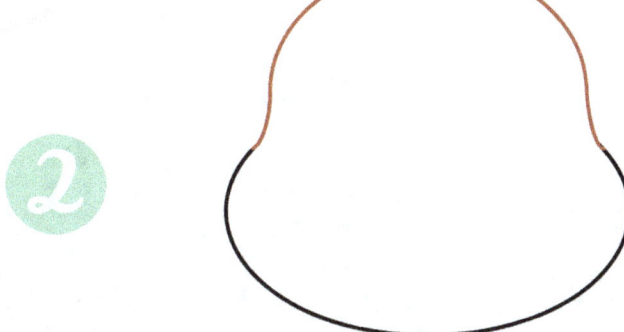

3

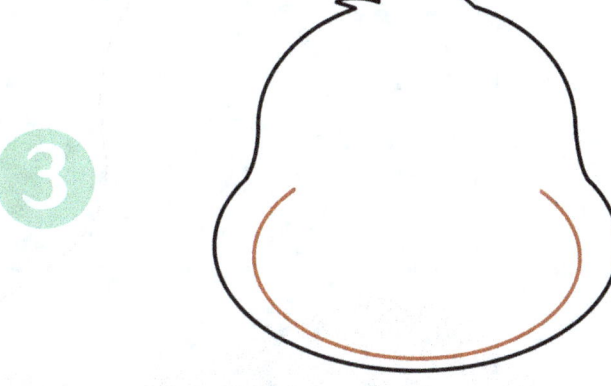

4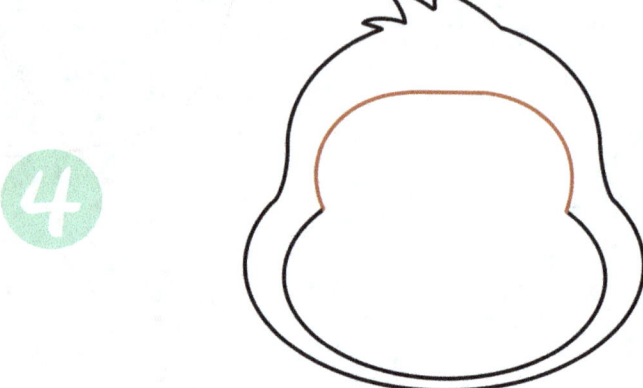

5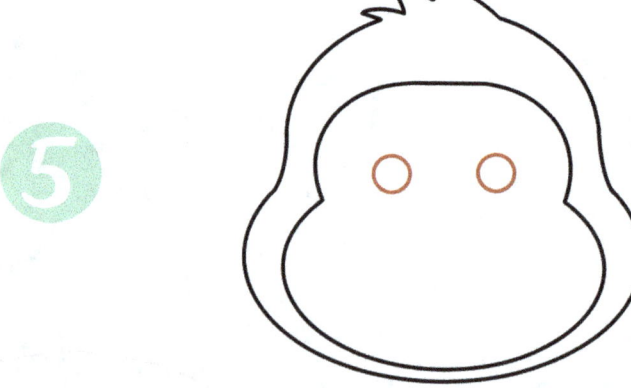

6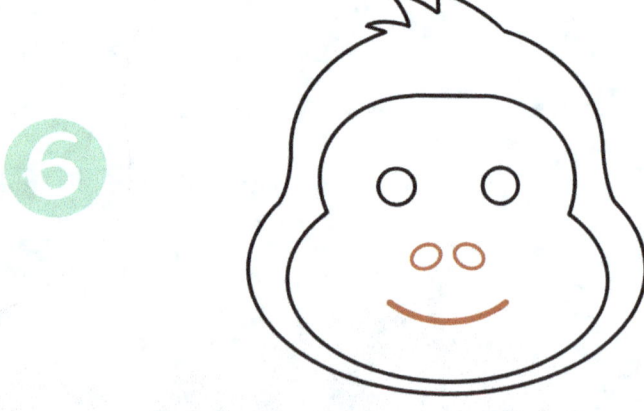

7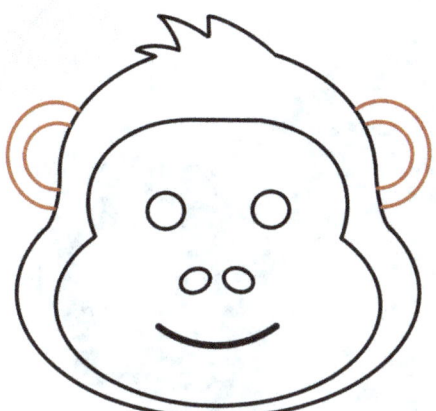

8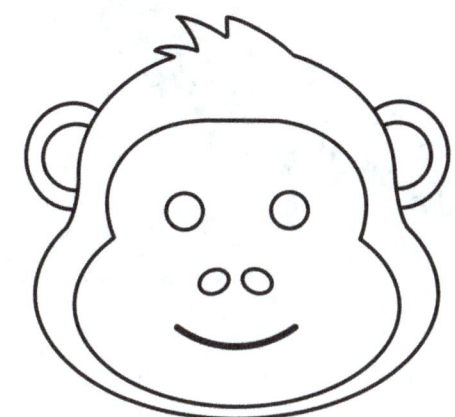

9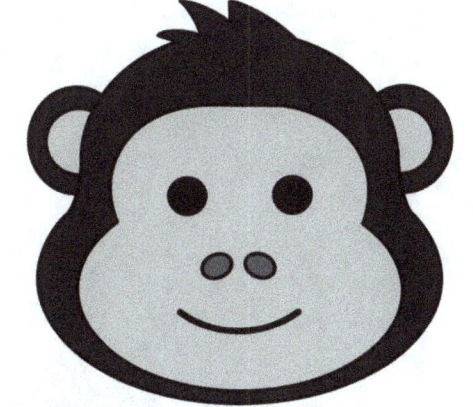

Gorilla

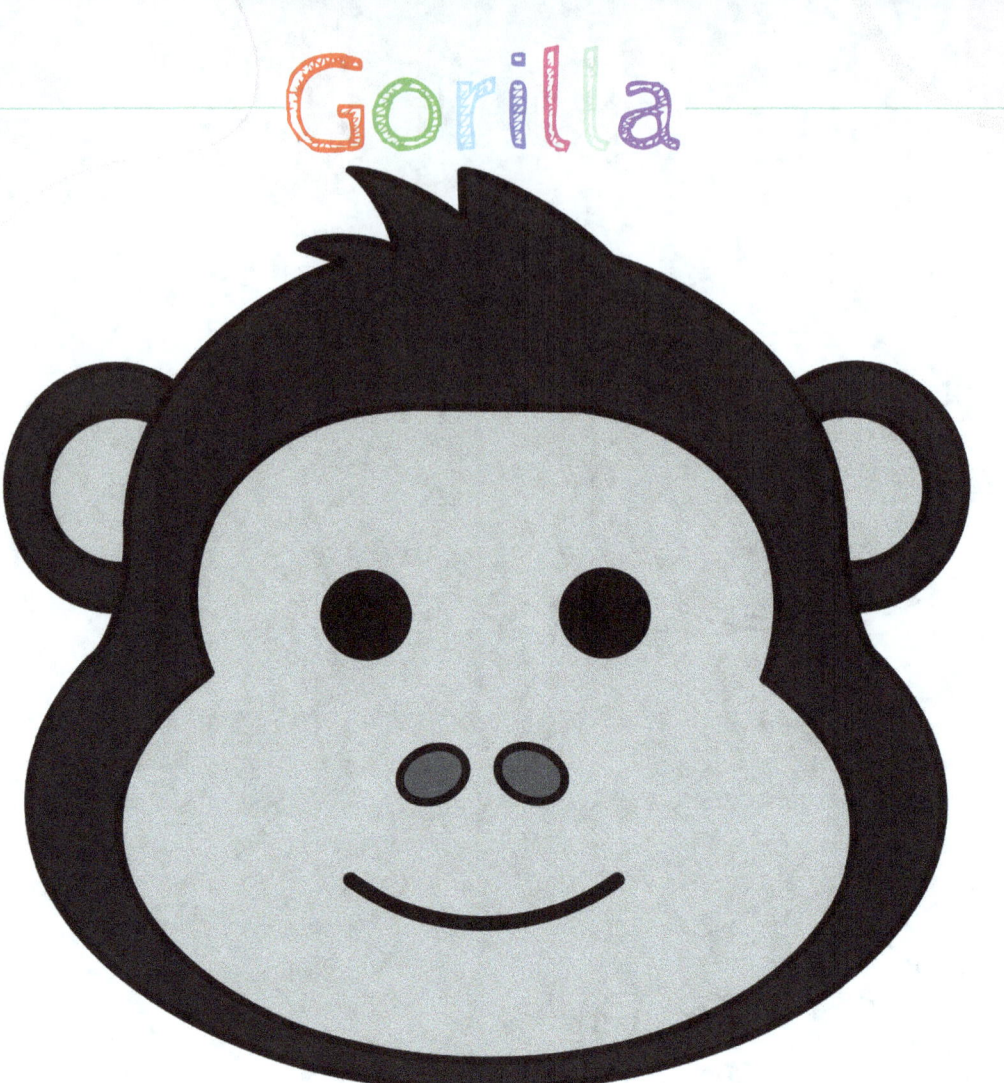

Snake

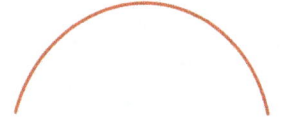

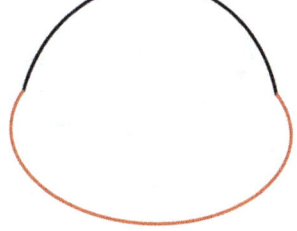

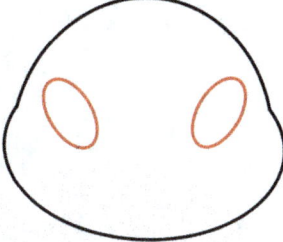

Snake

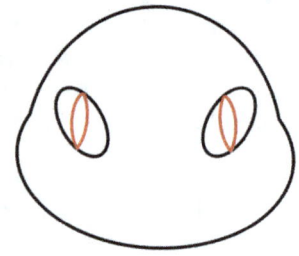

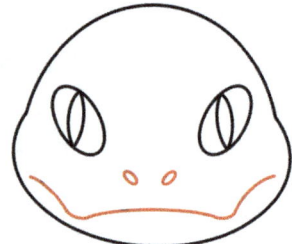

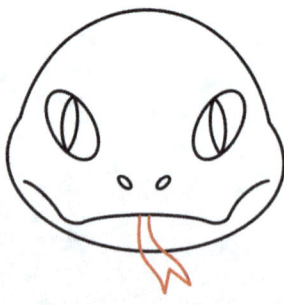

Snake

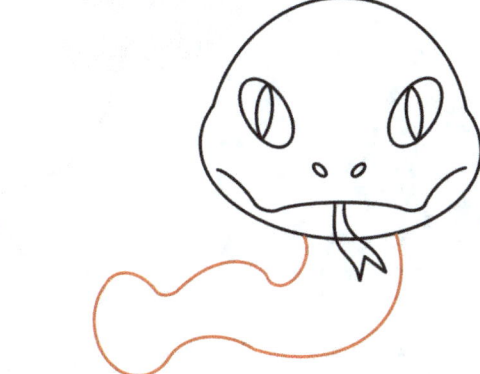

7

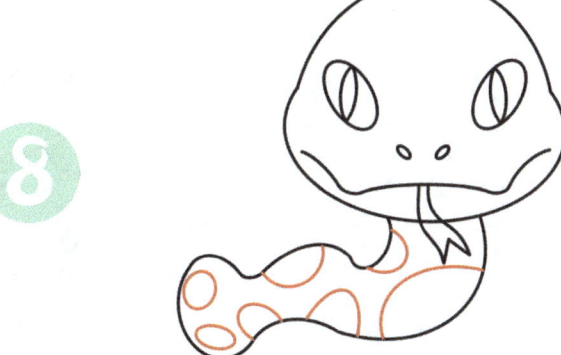

8

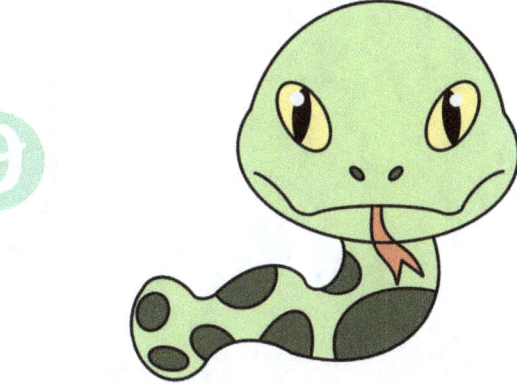

9

Snake

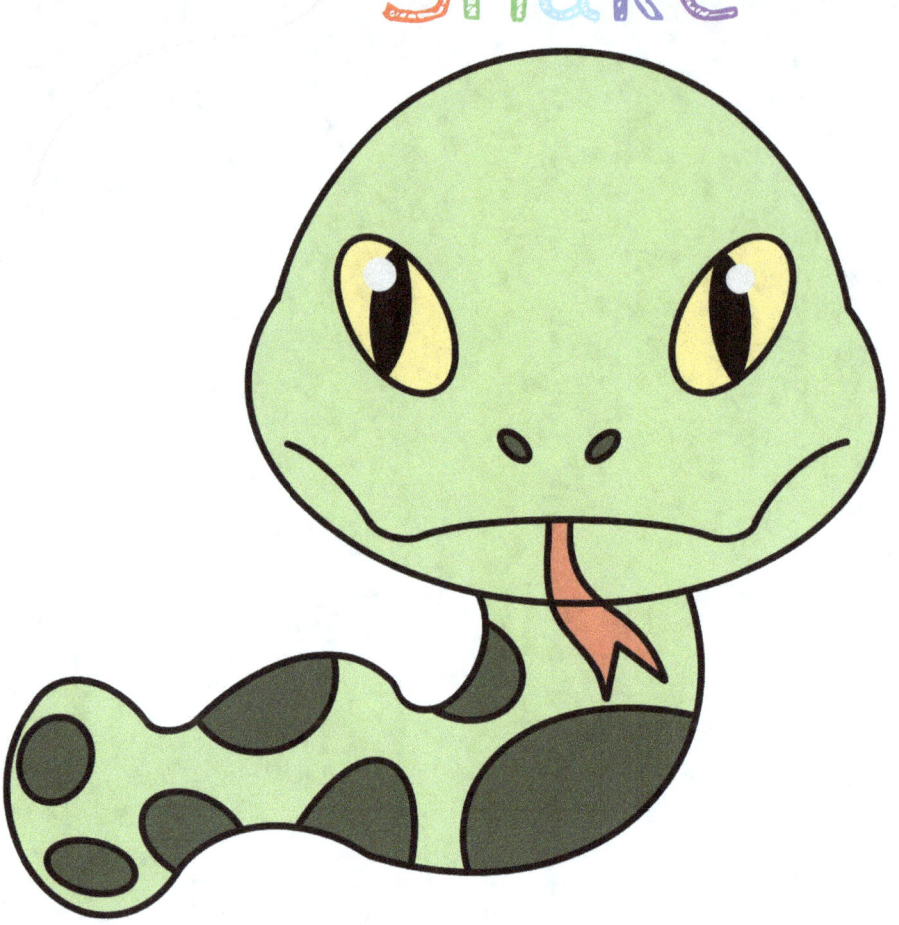

Elephant

1

2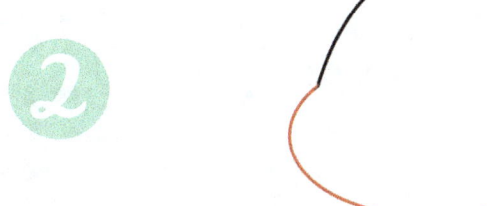

3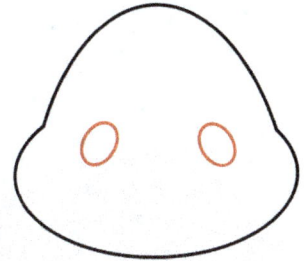

Elephant

 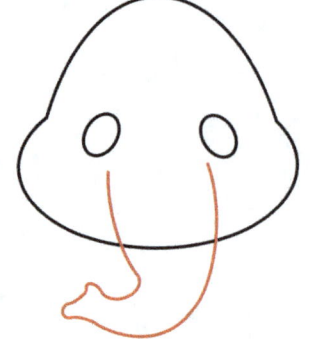

 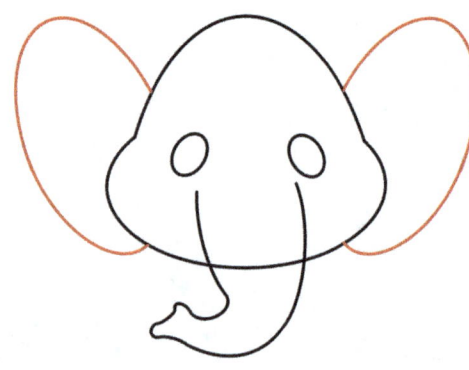

 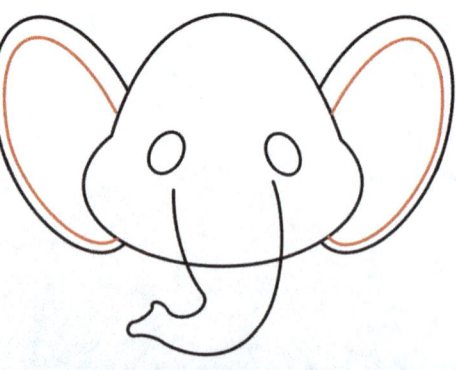

Elephant

7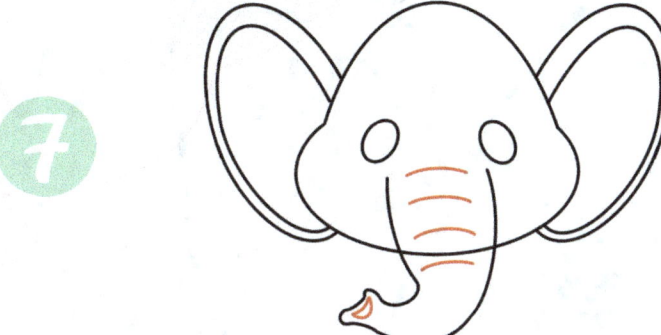

8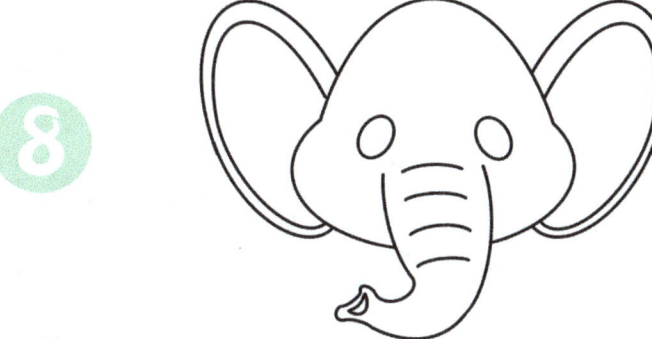

9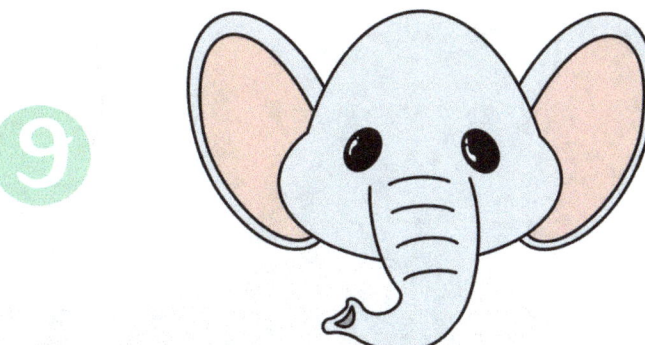

Elephant

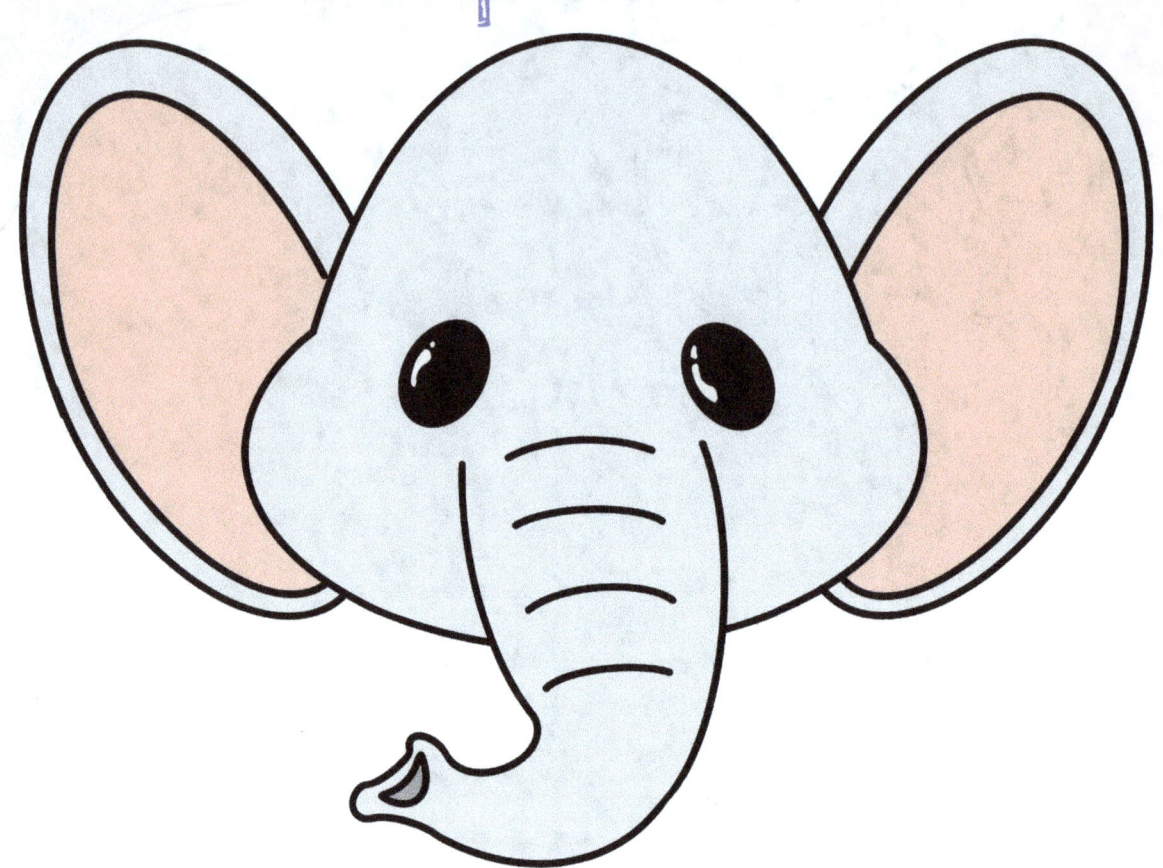

Elephant

Giraffe

 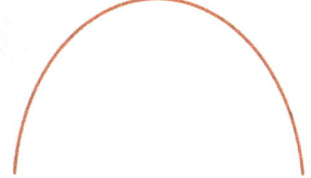

 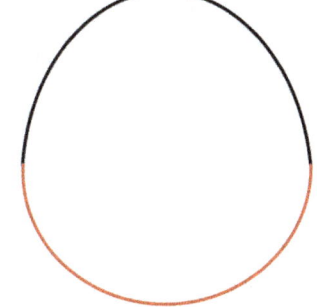

 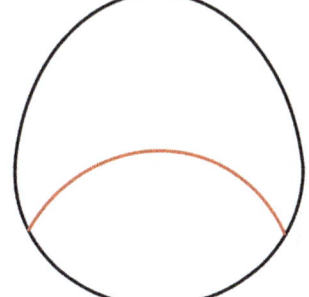

 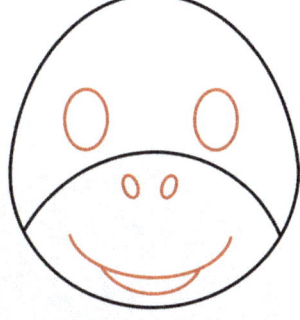

Giraffe

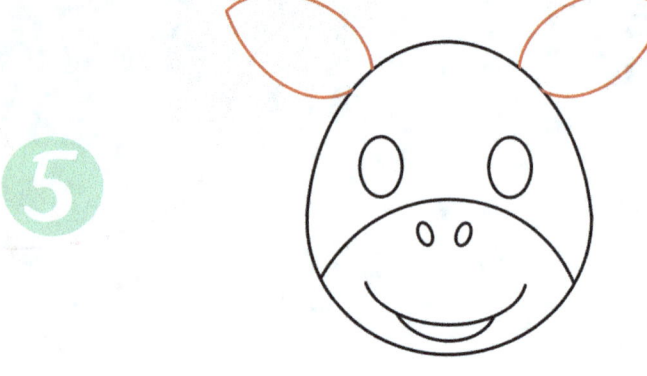

5

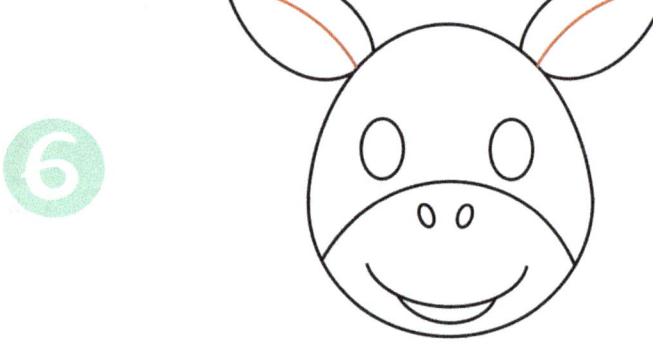

6

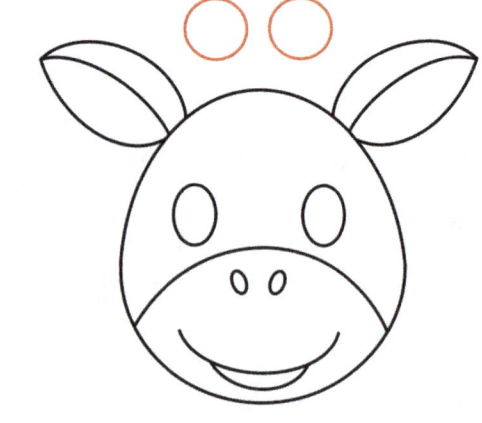

7

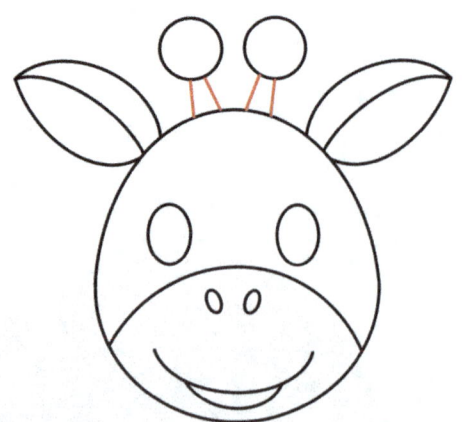

8

Giraffe

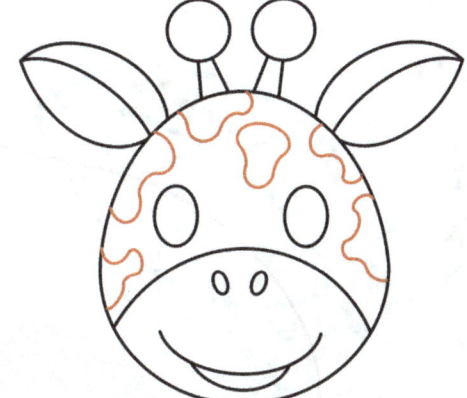

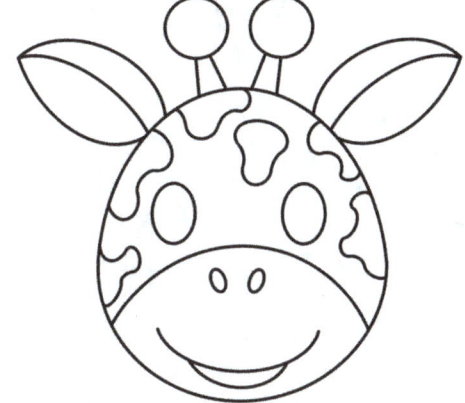

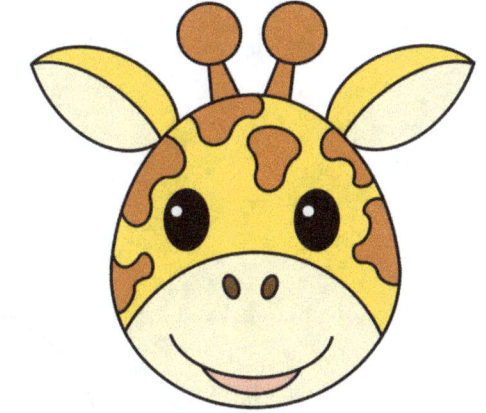

Giraffe

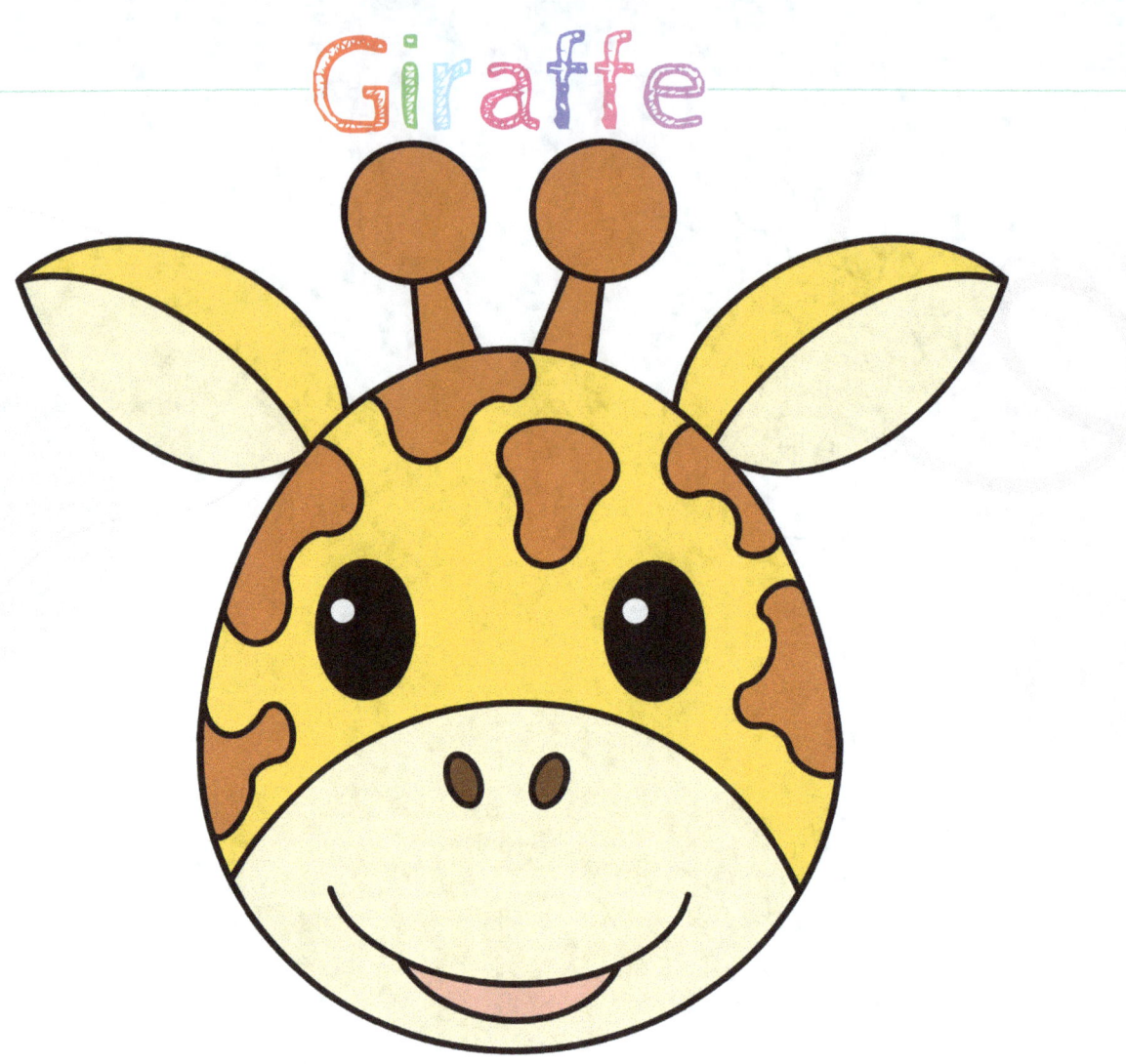

Clown Fish

1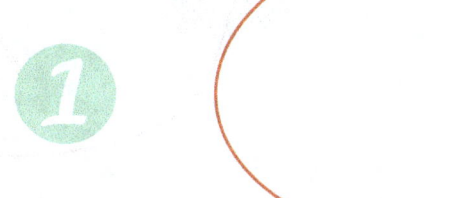

2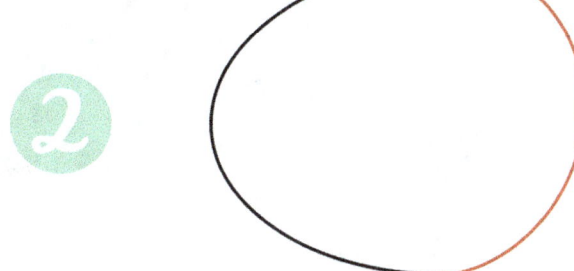

3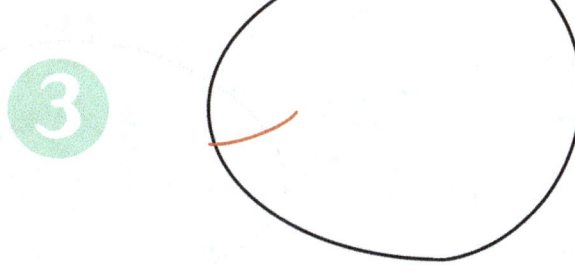

4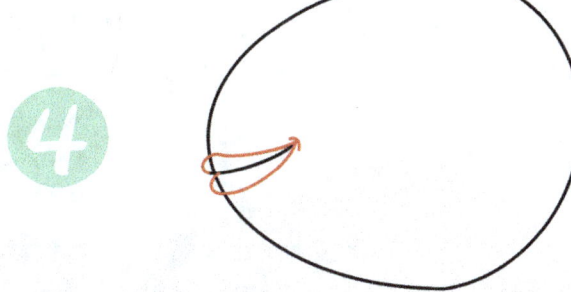

Clown Fish

5

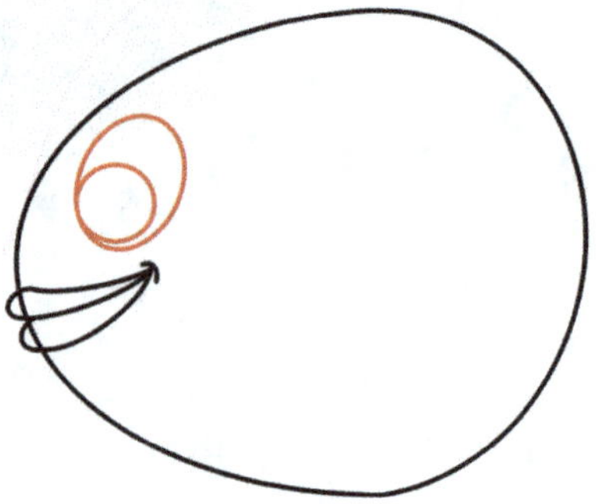

6

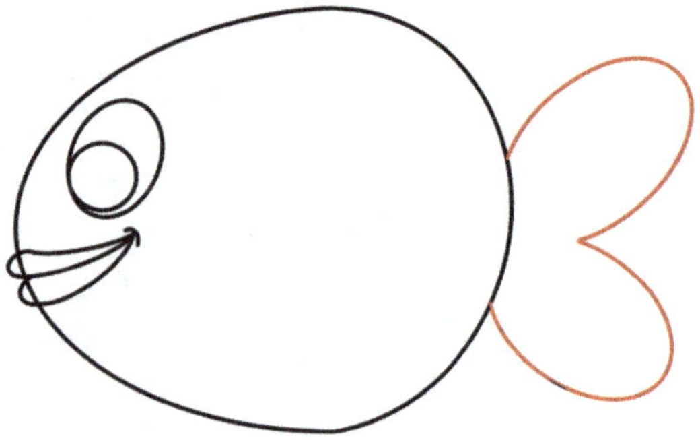

7

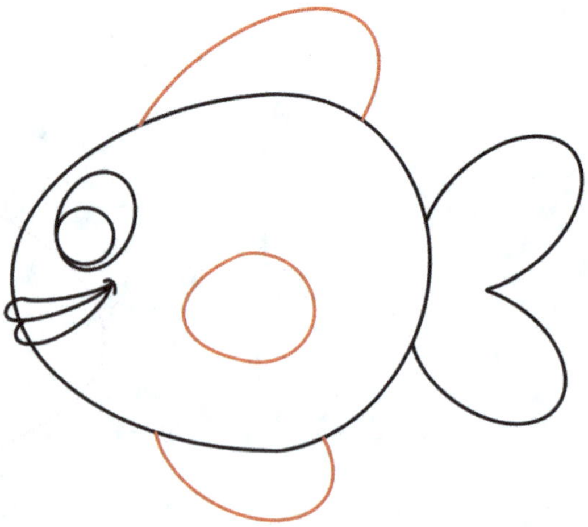

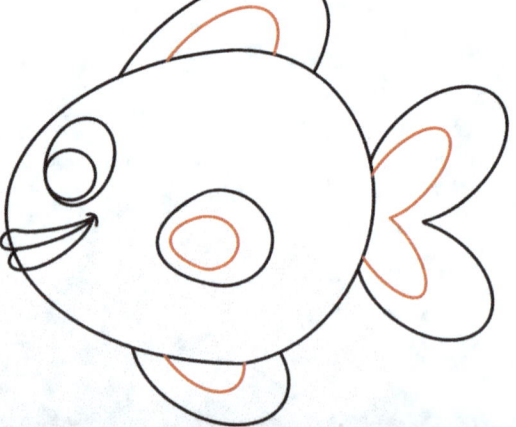

Clown Fish

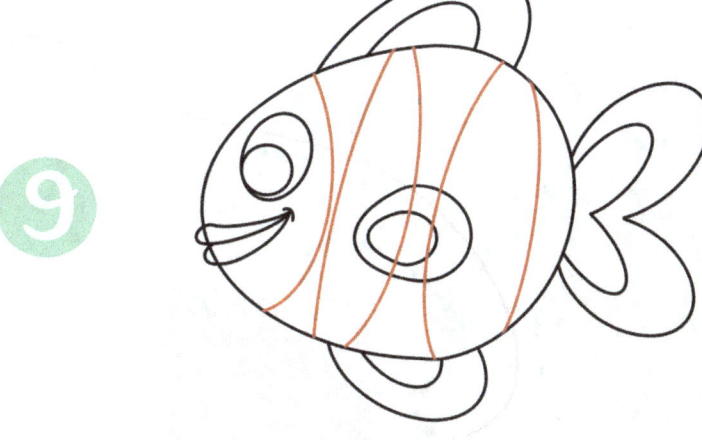

9

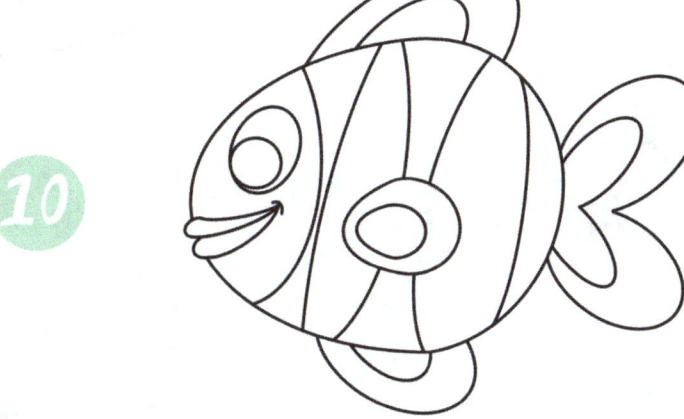

10

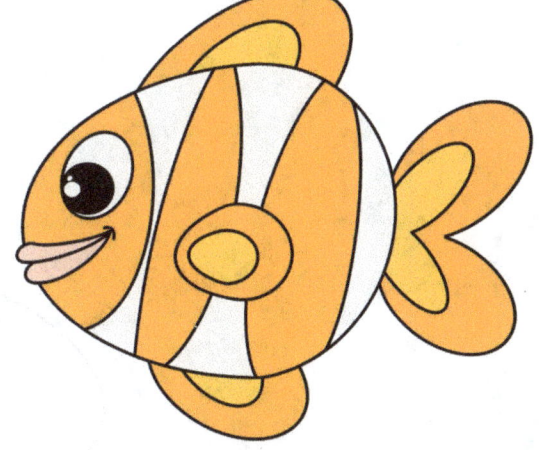

11

Clown Fish

Dolphin

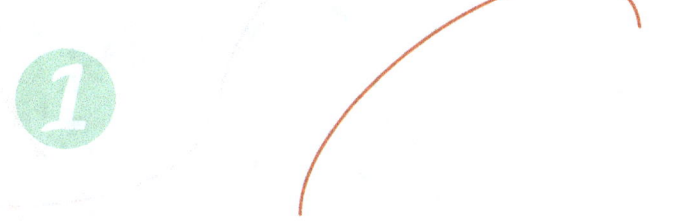

1

2

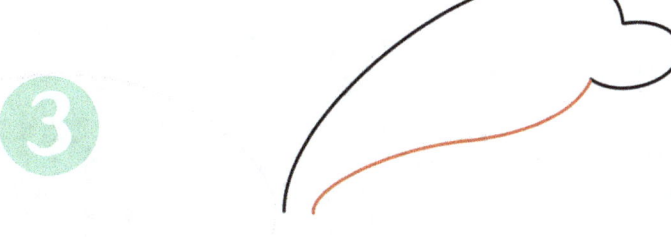

3

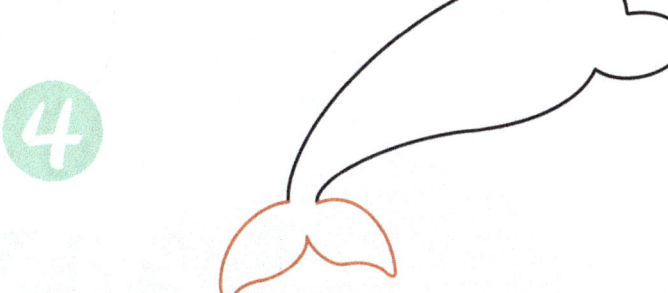

4

Dolphin

5

6

7

Dolphin

8

9

10

Dolphin

11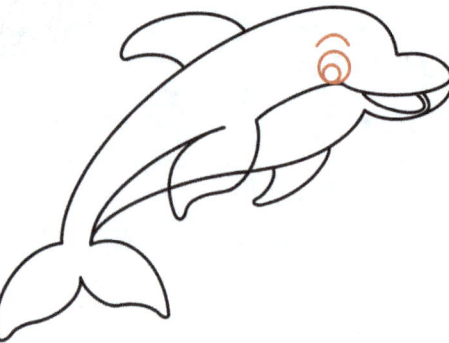

12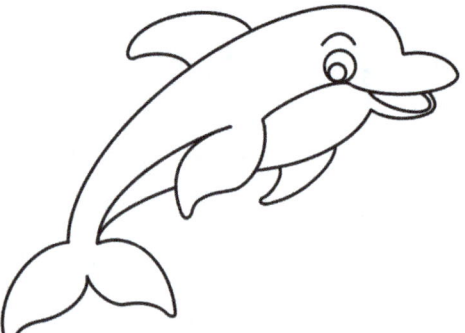

13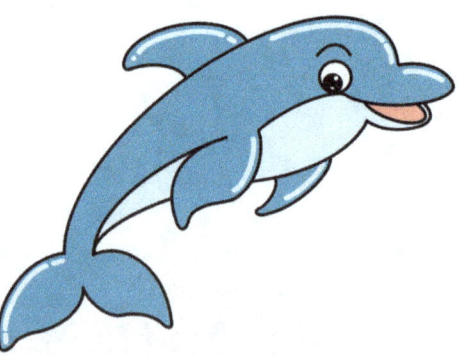

Dolphin

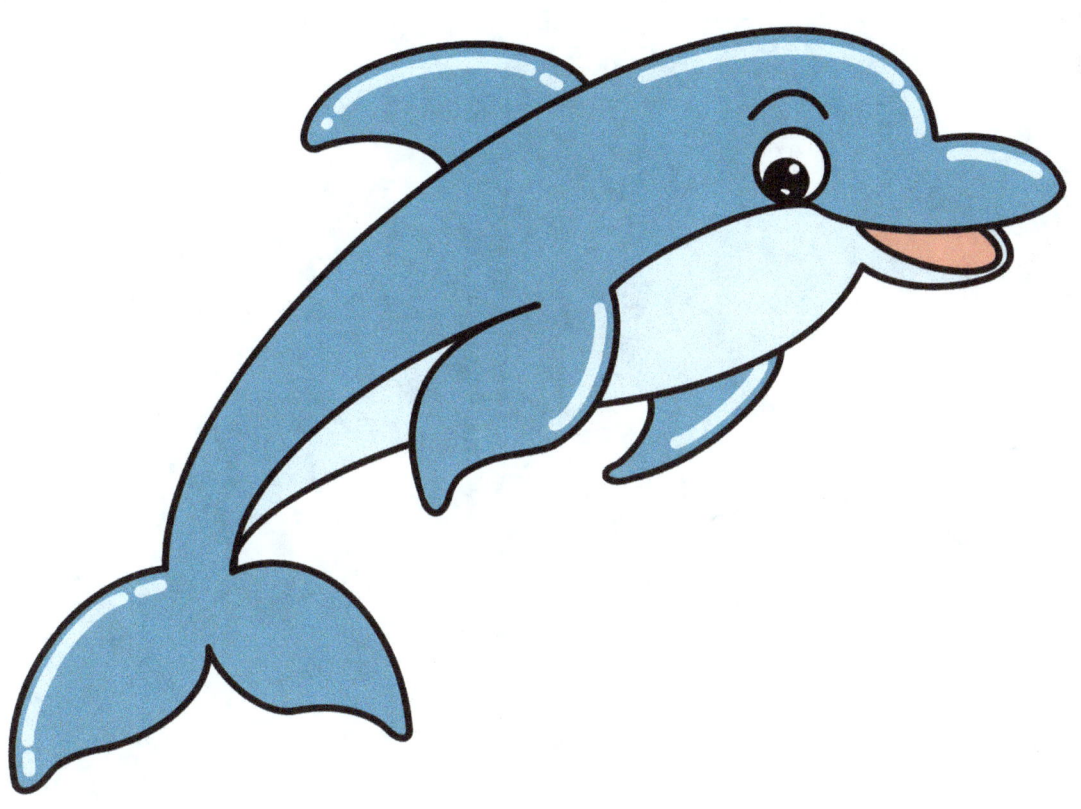

Dolphin

Sea Turtle

1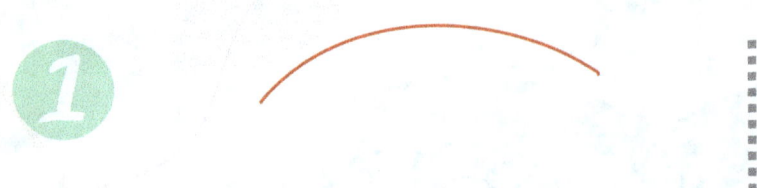

2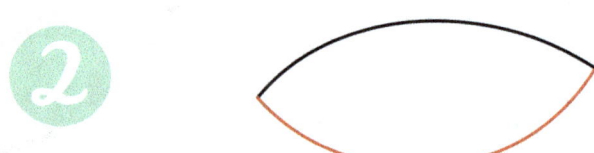

3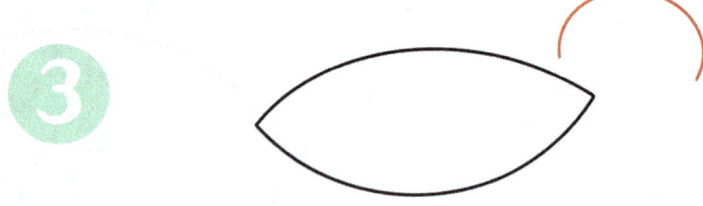

4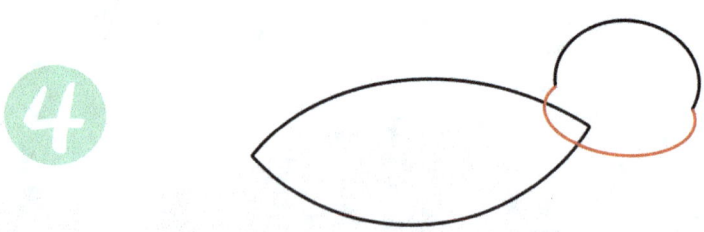

Sea Turtle

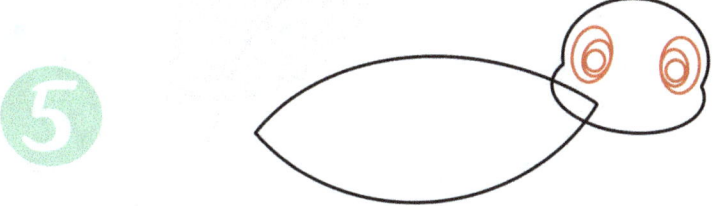

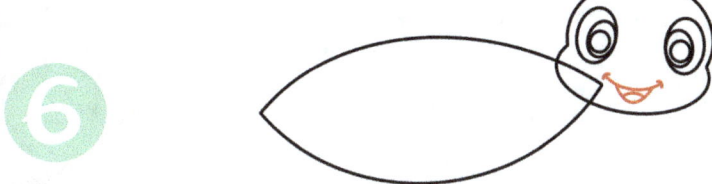

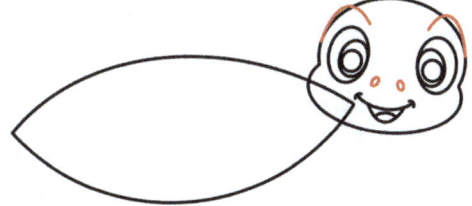

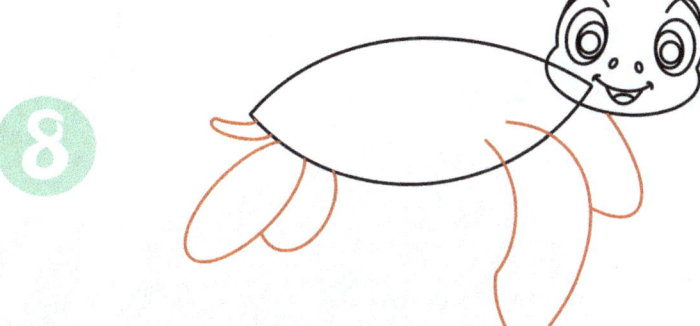

Sea Turtle

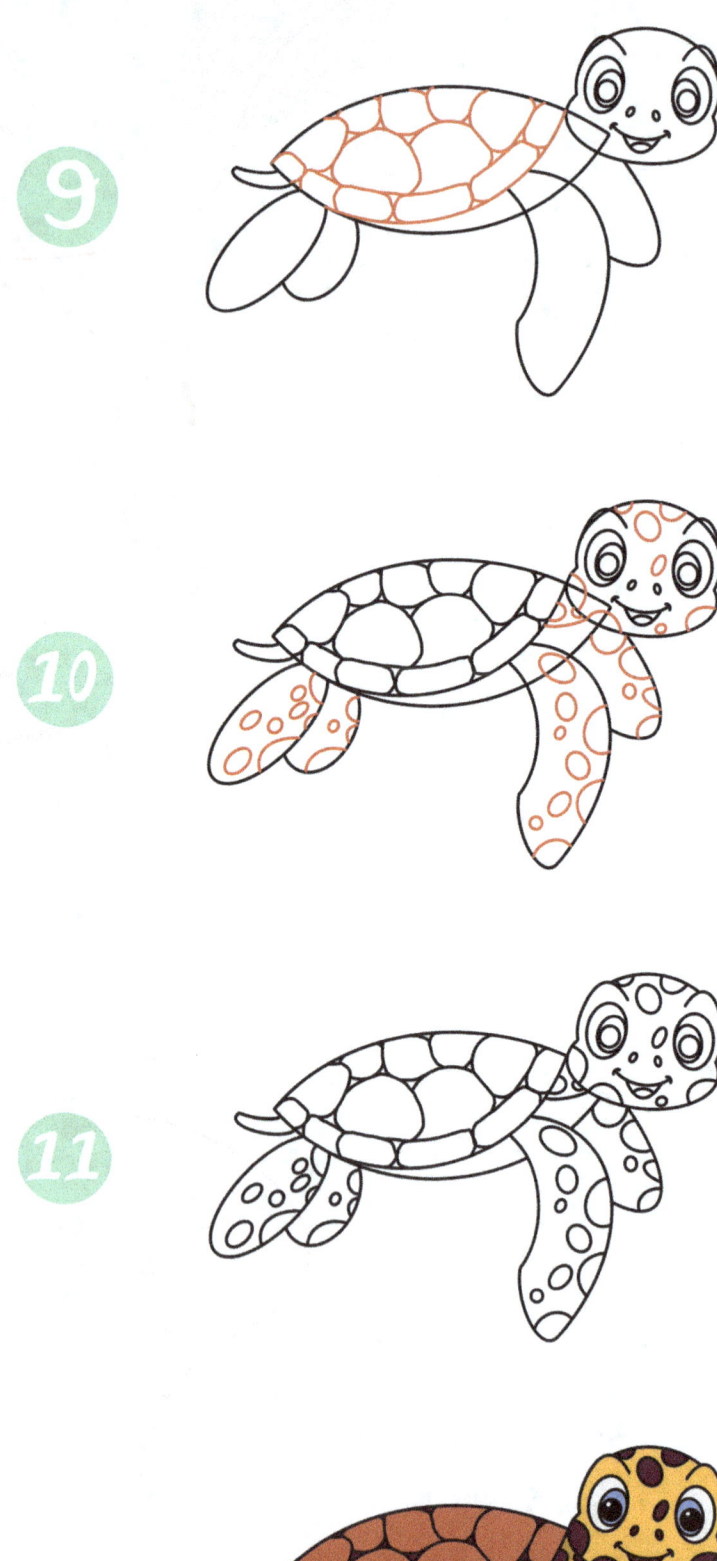

9

10

11

12

Sea Turtle

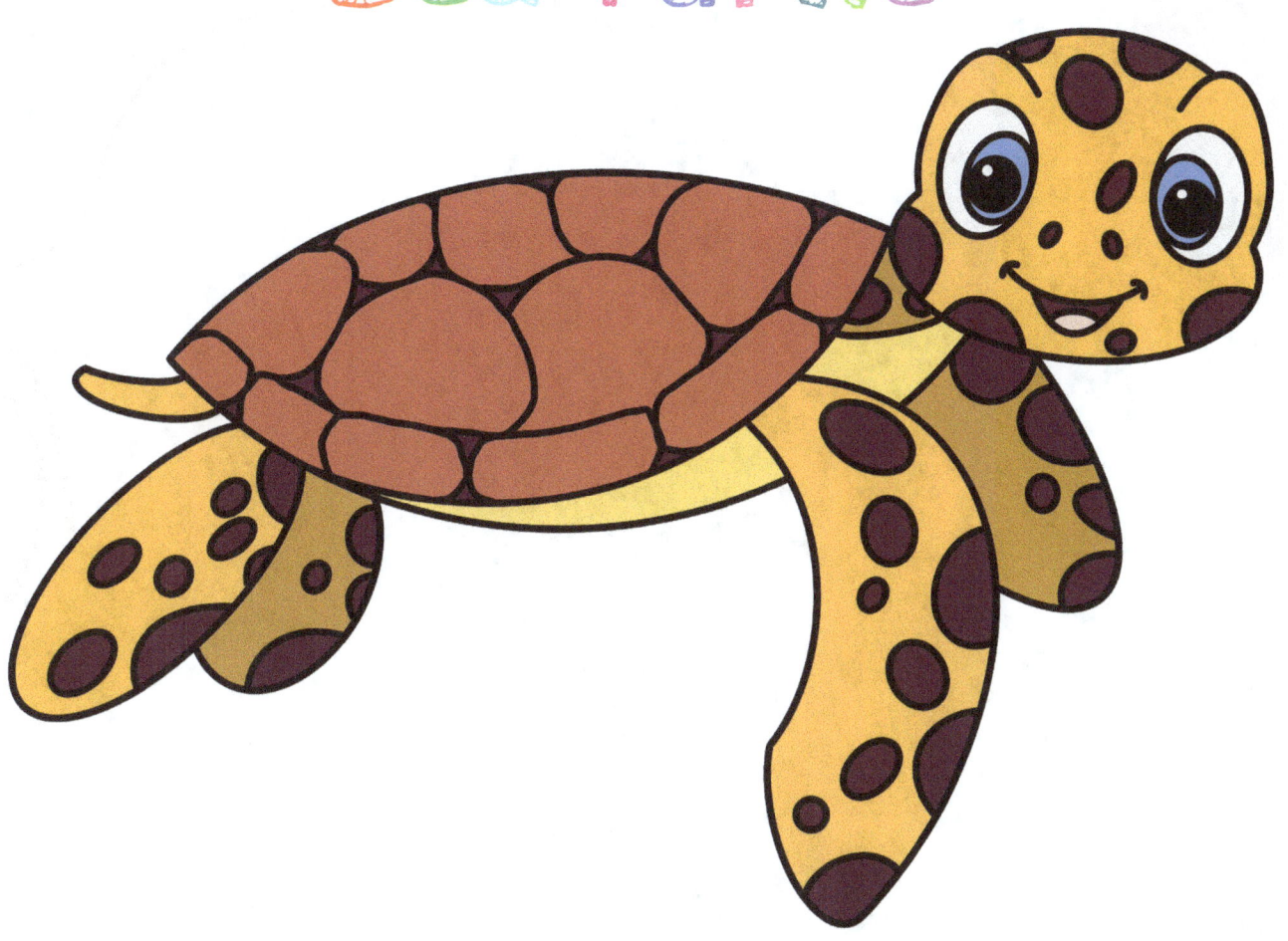

Octopus

1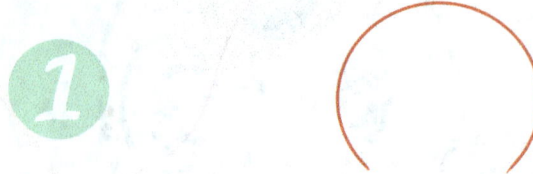

2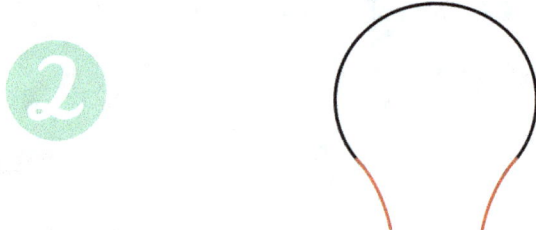

3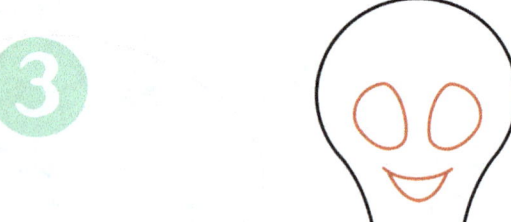

4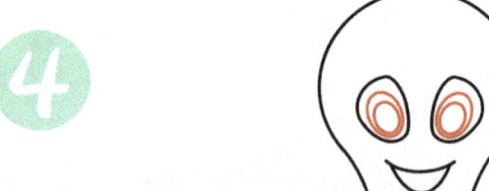

Octopus

5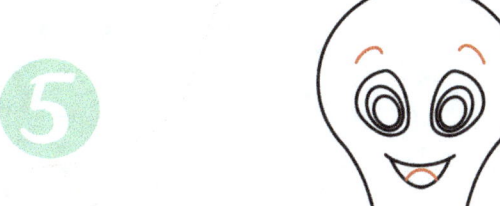

6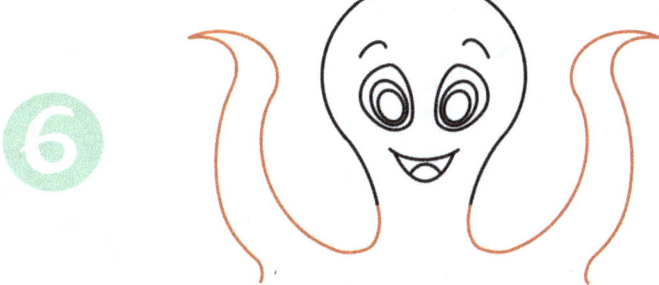

7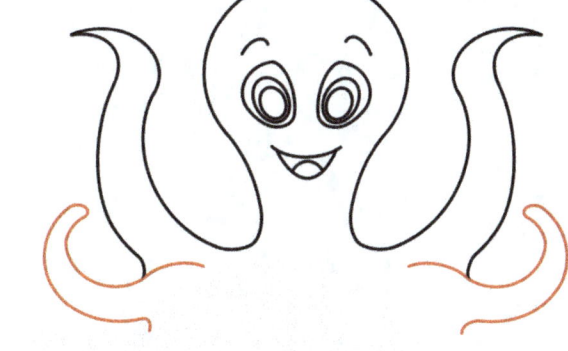

Octopus

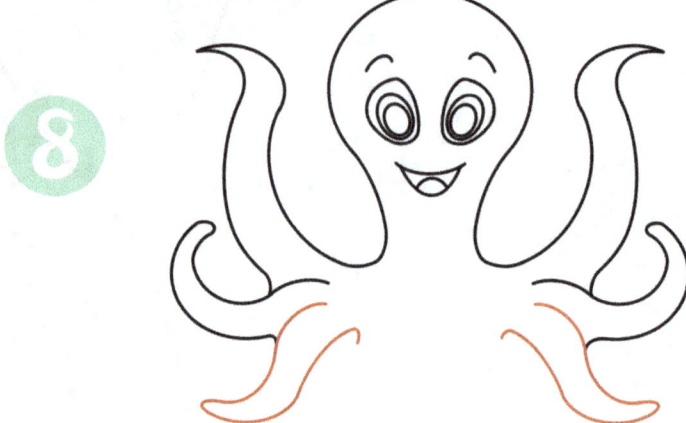

8

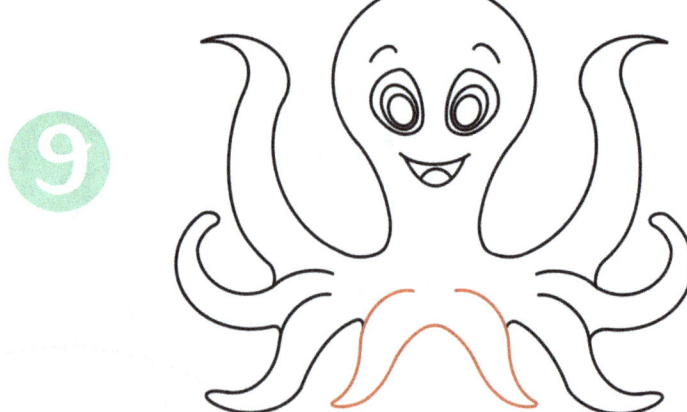

9

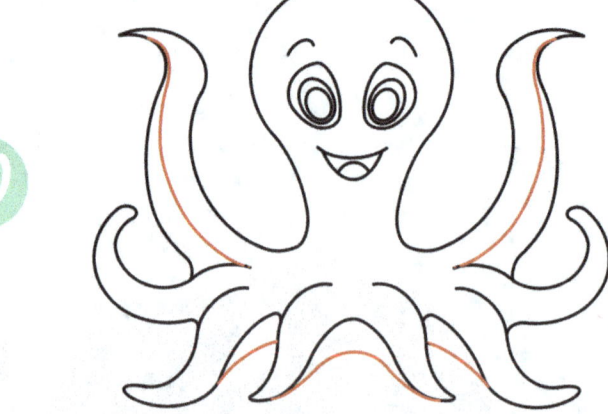

10

Octopus

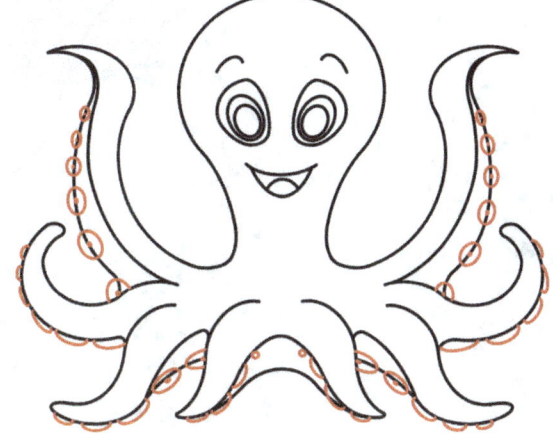

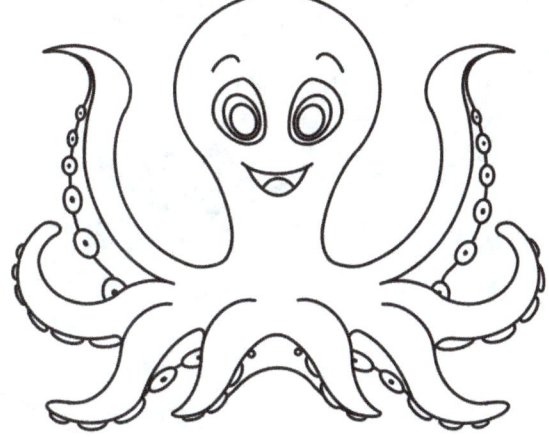

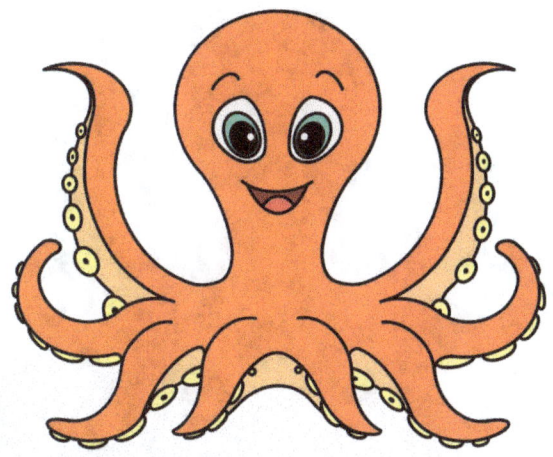

Octopus

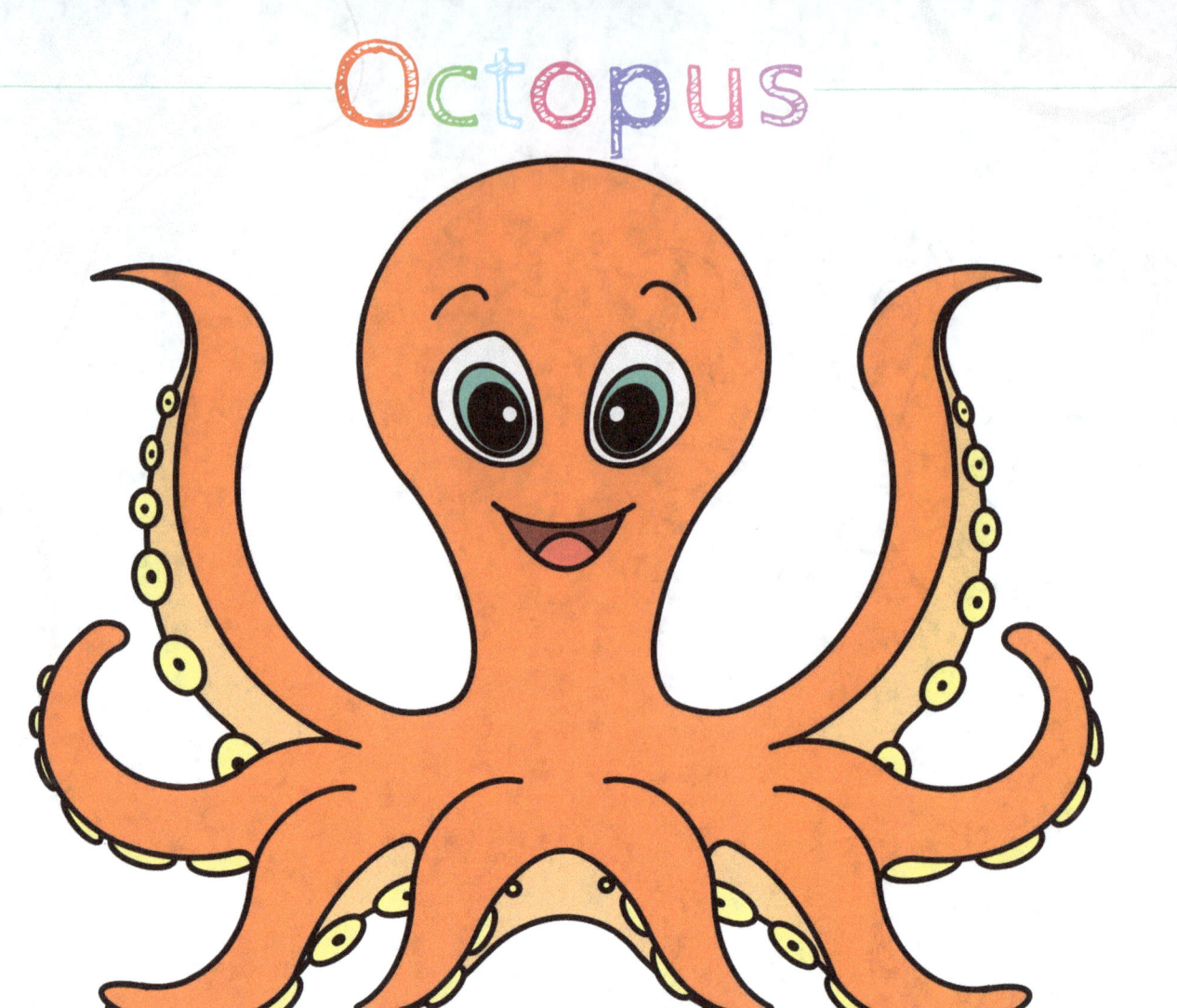

Cow

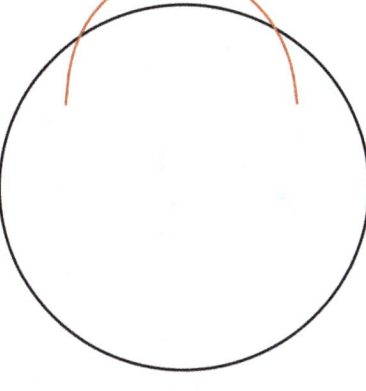

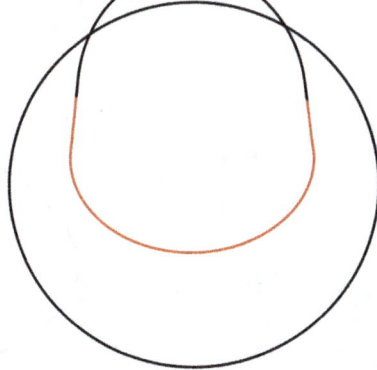

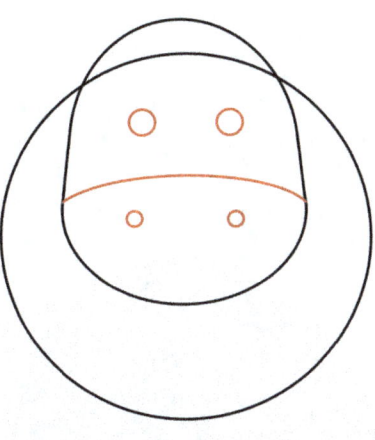

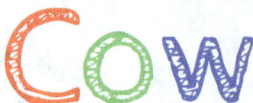

Cow

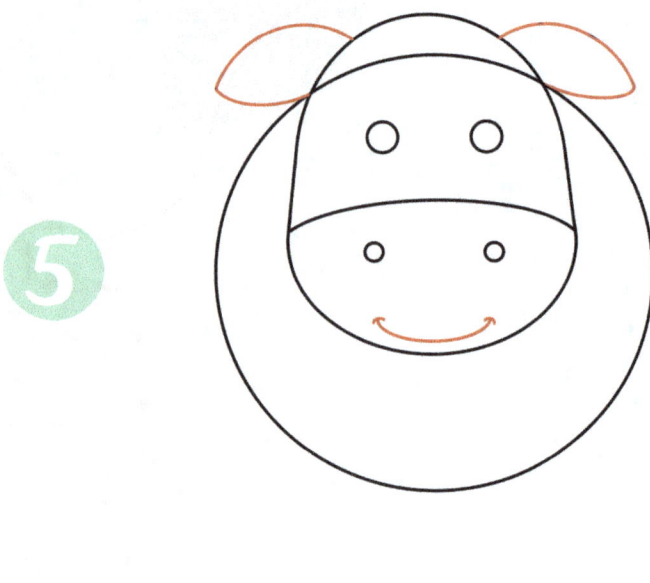

5

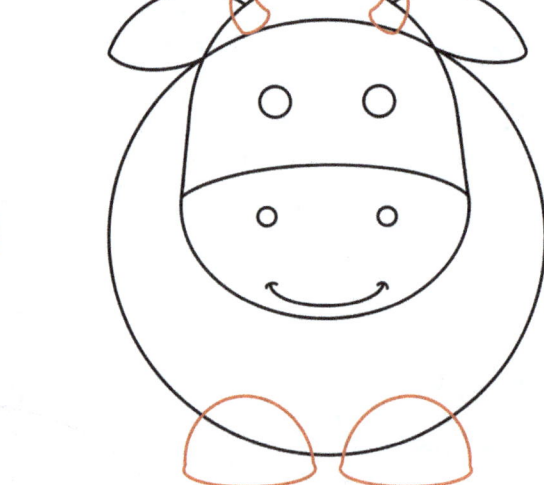

6

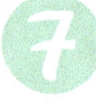 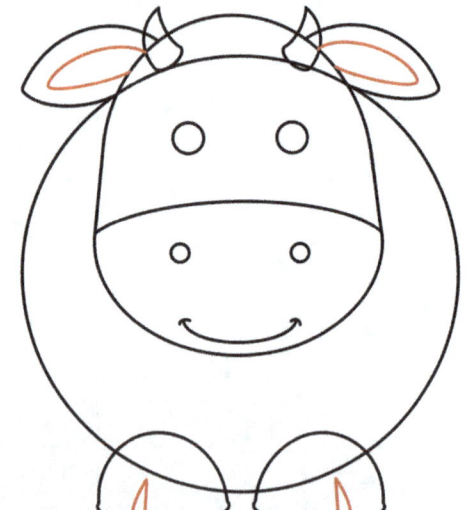

7

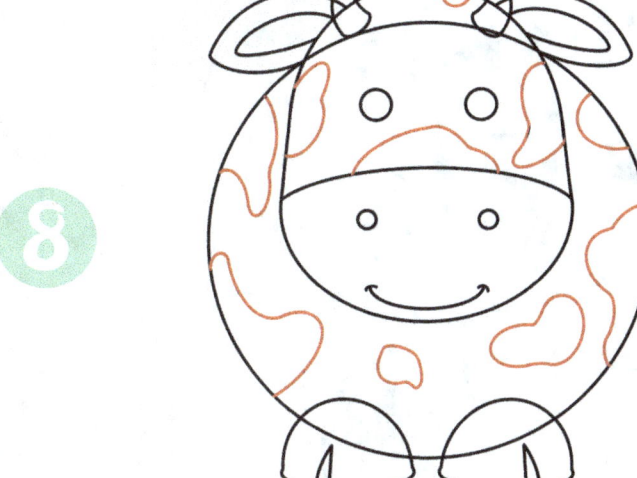

8

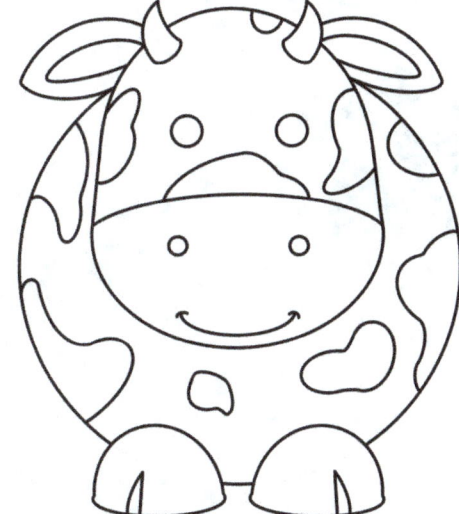

9

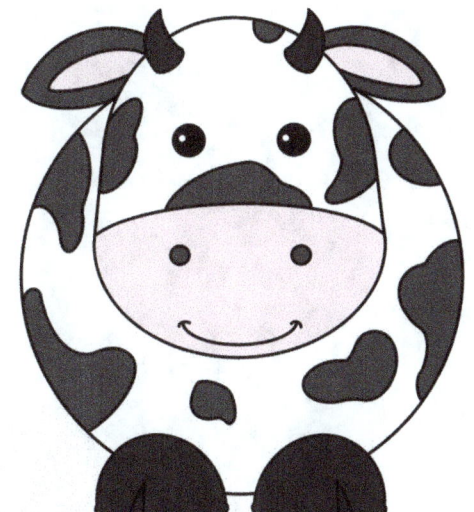

10

Cow

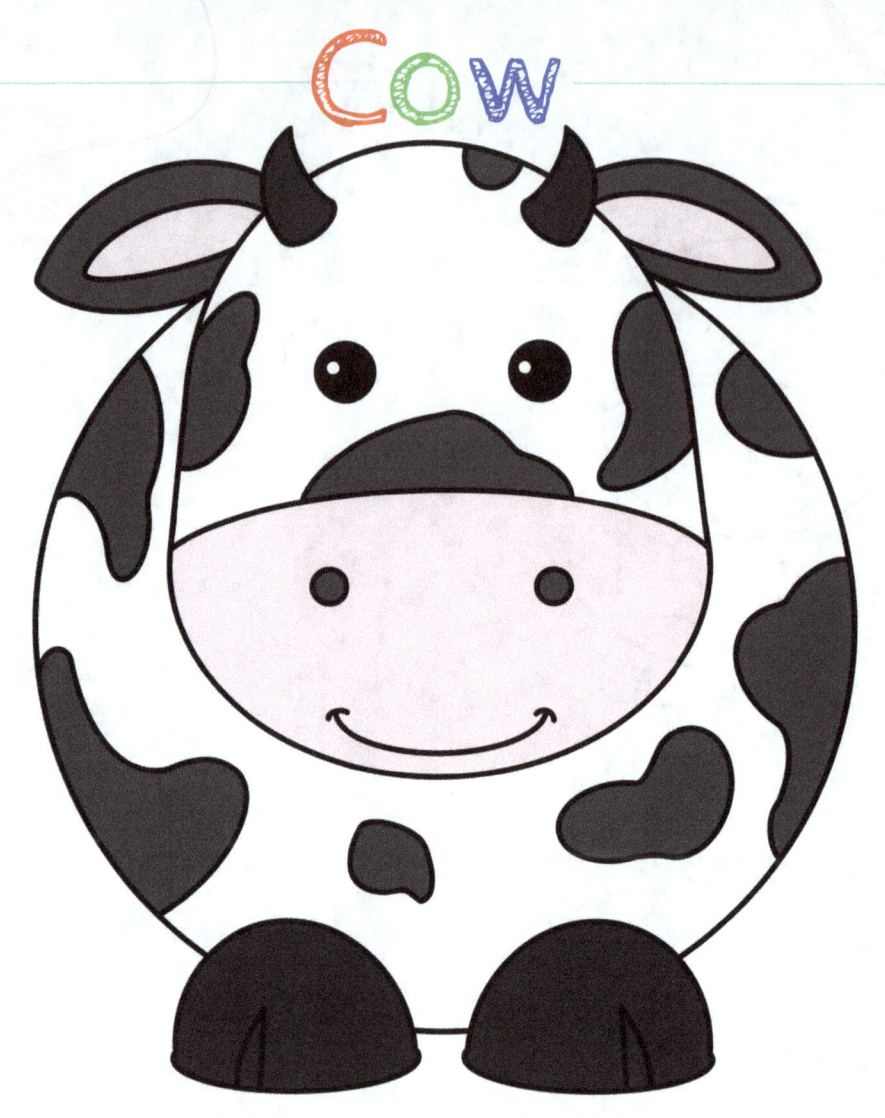

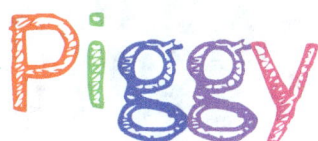

1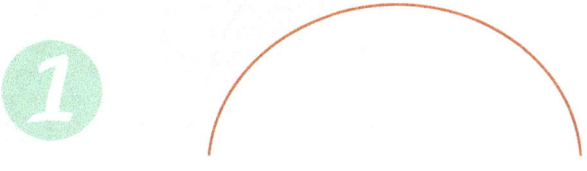

2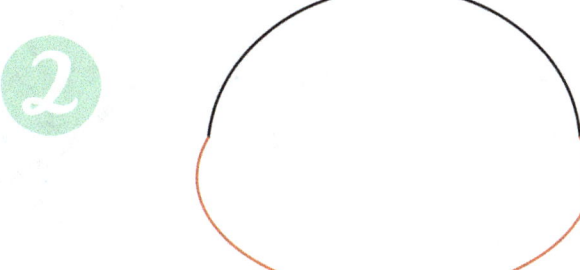

3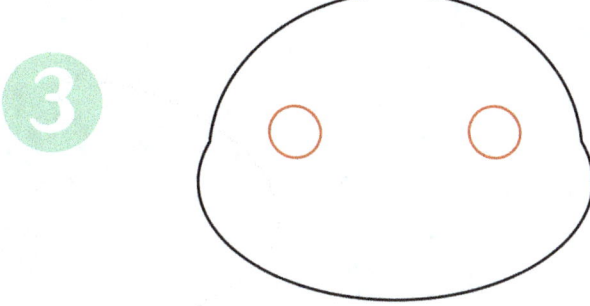

4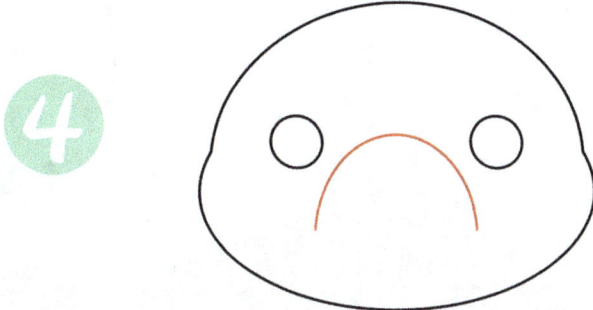

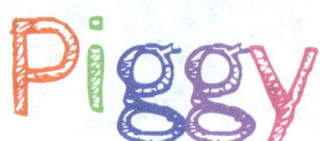

⑤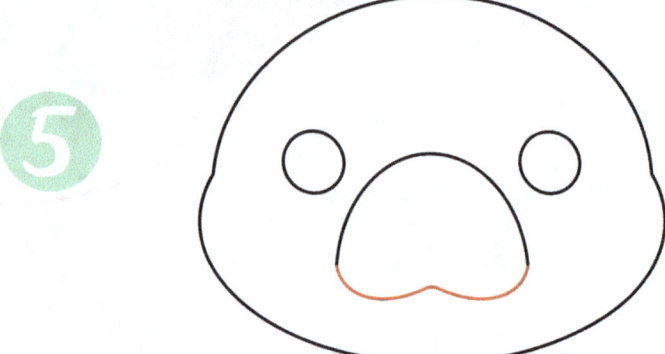

⑥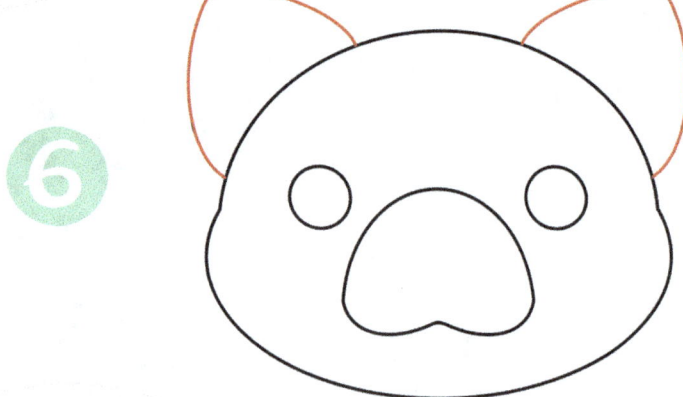

⑦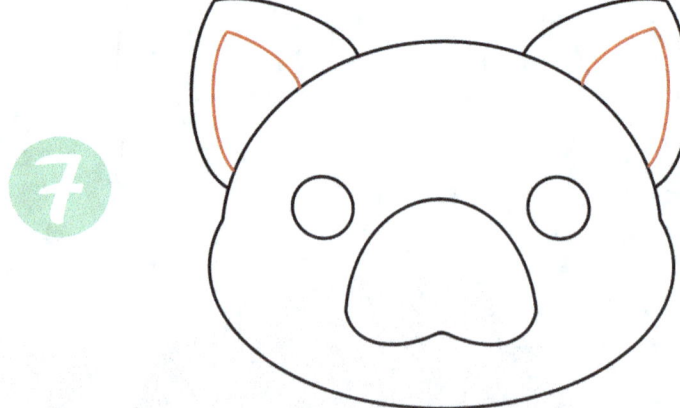

Piggy

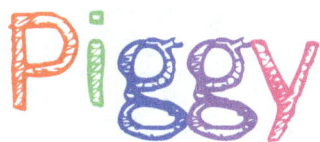

8

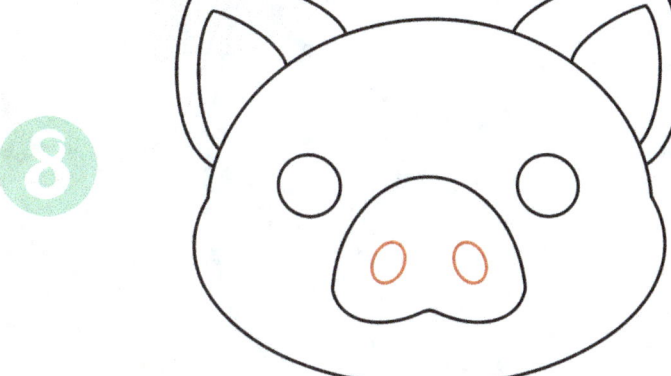

9

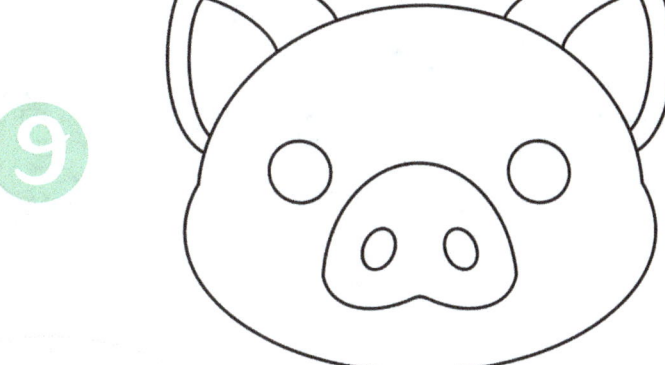

10

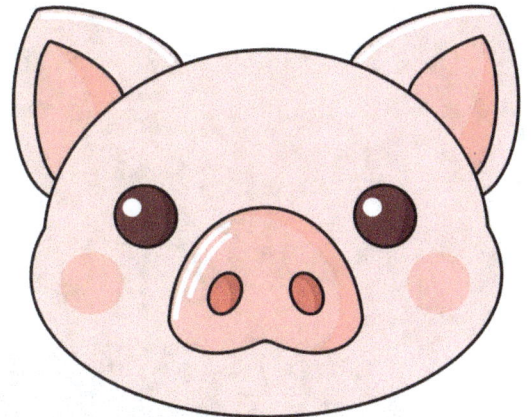

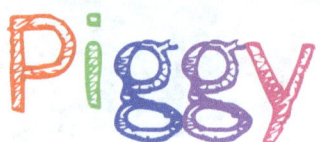

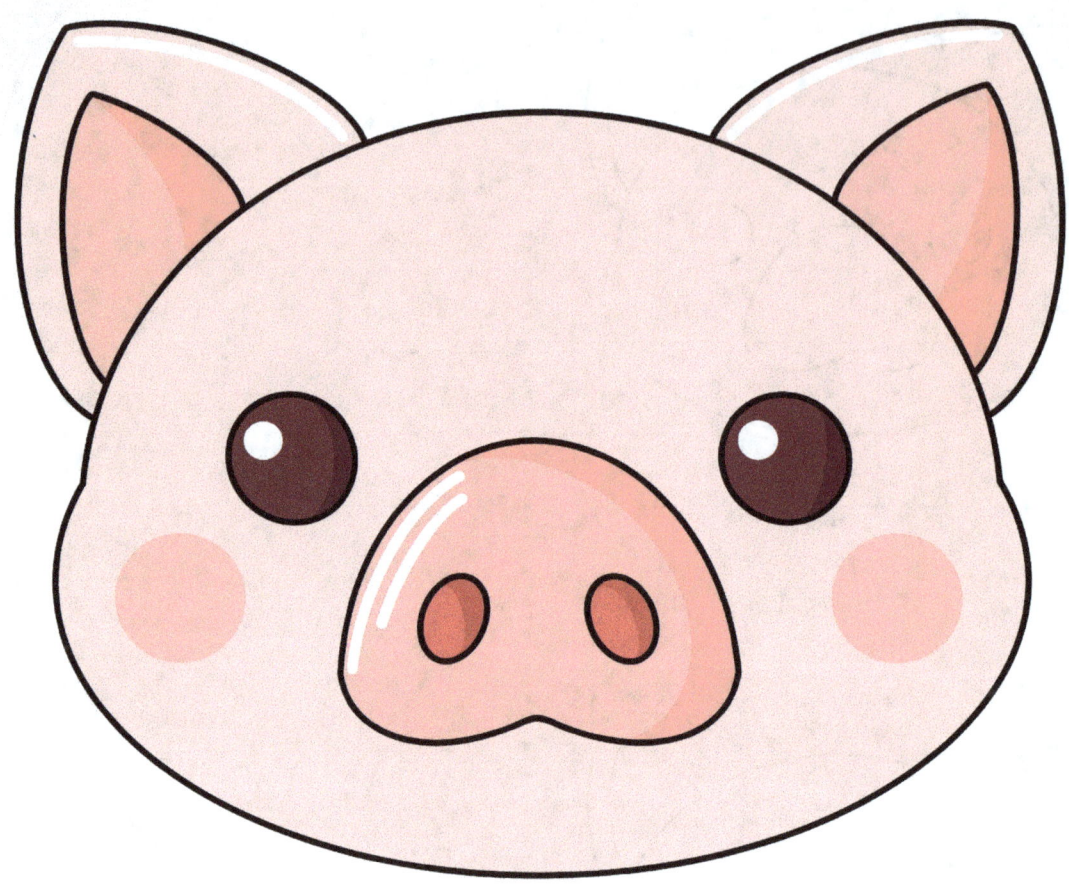

Chicken

1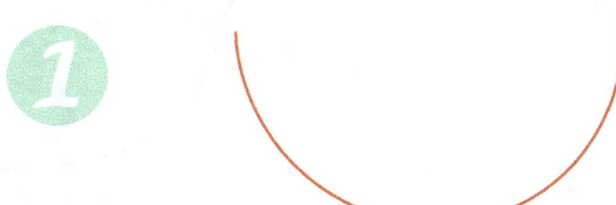

2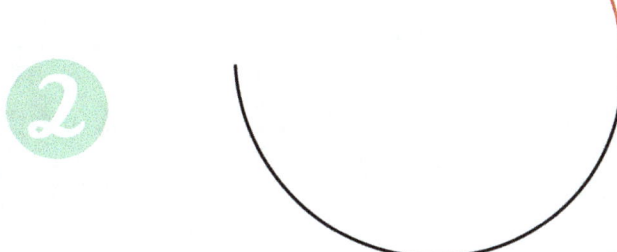

3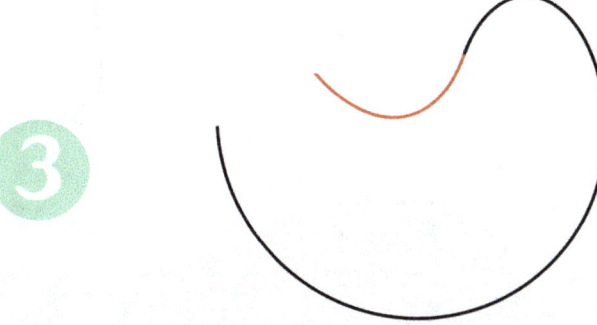

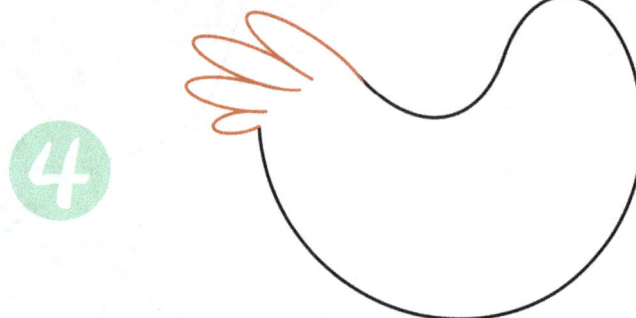

4

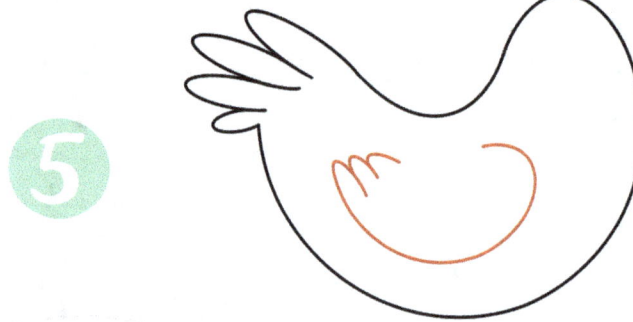

5

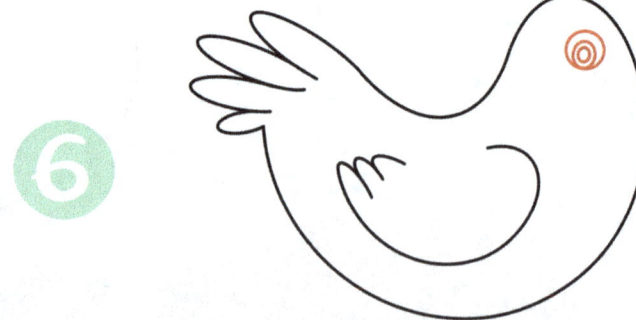

6

Chicken

7

8

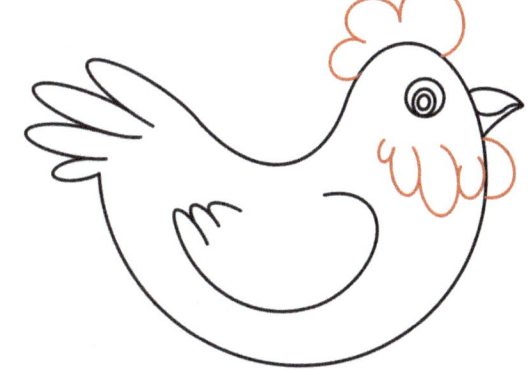

9

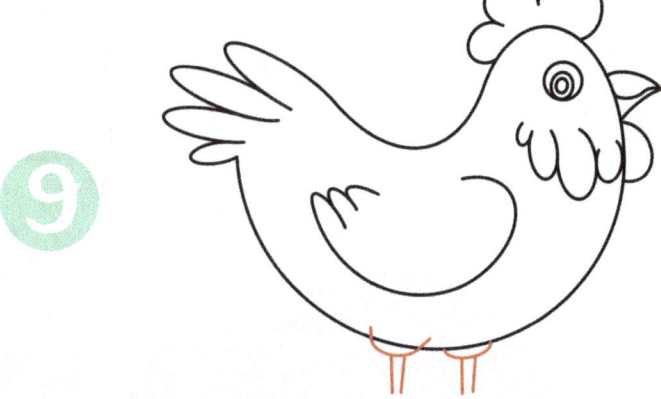

Chicken

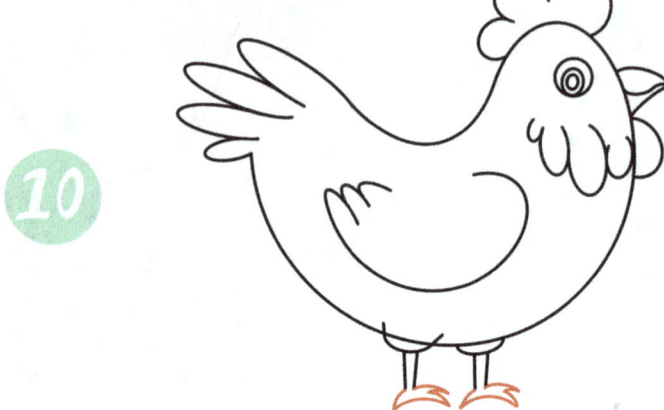

10

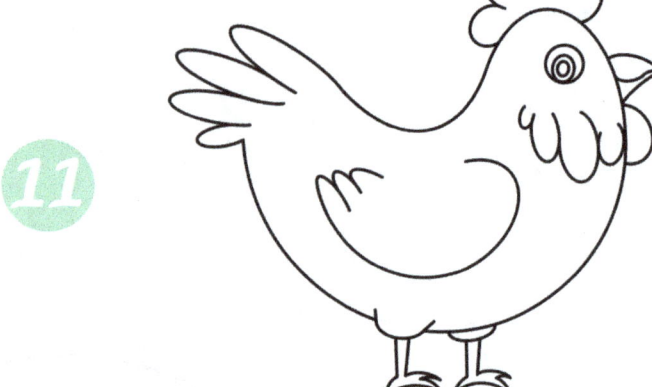

11

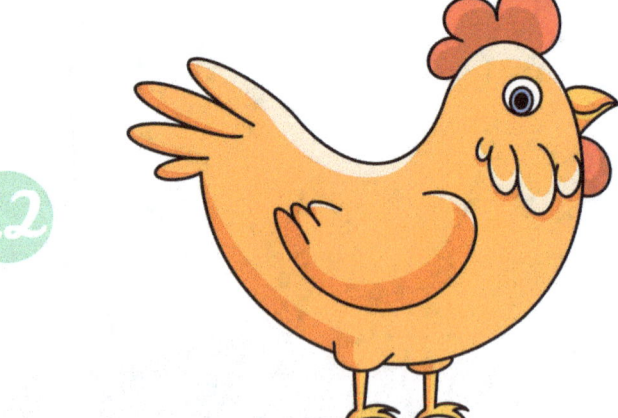

12

Chicken

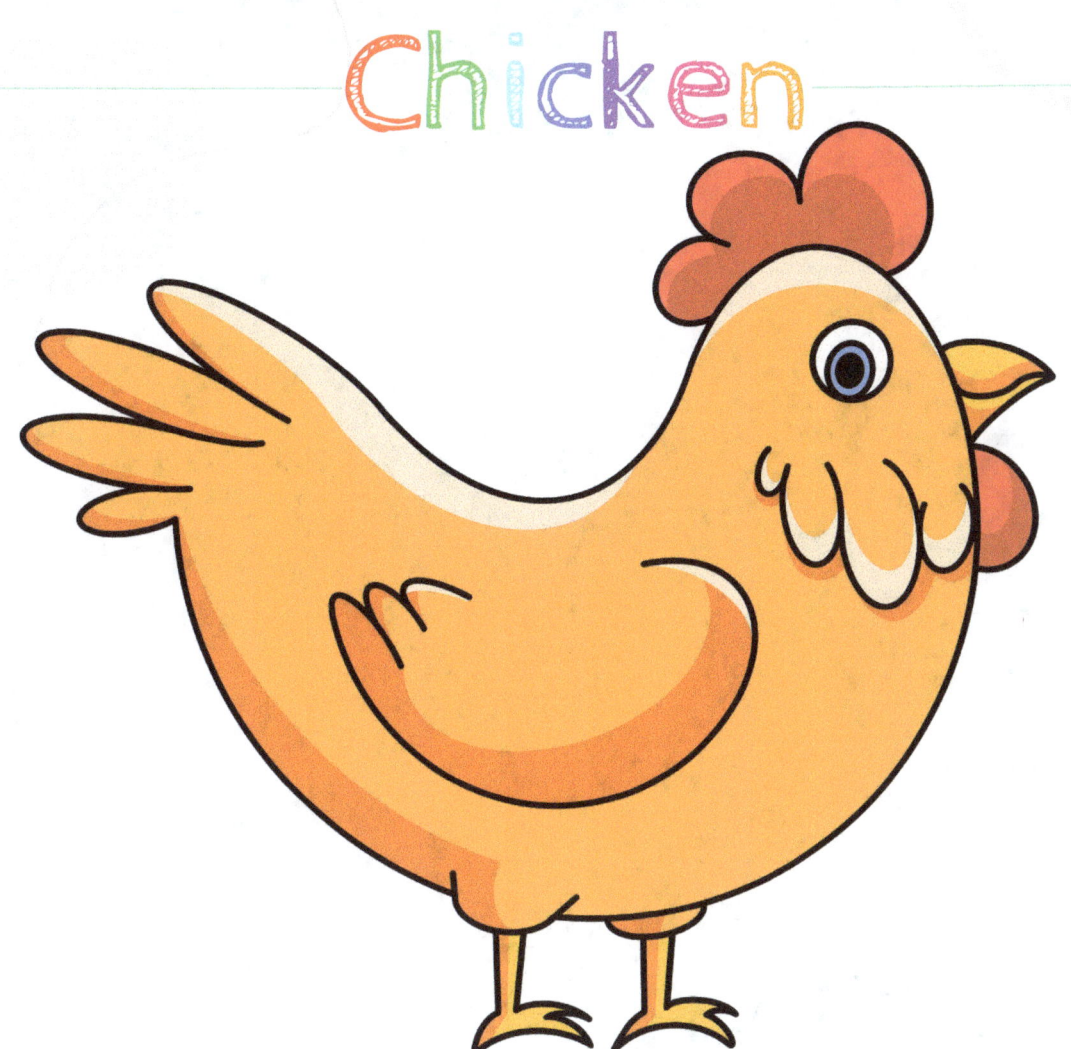

Chicken

Sheep

1

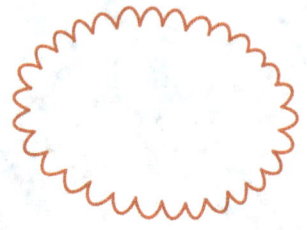

2

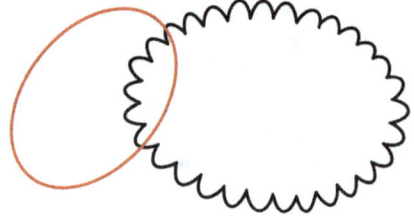

3

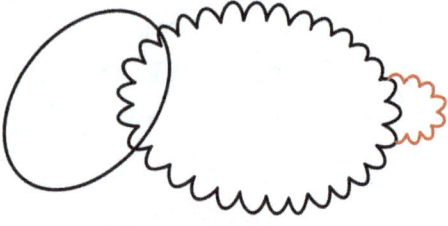

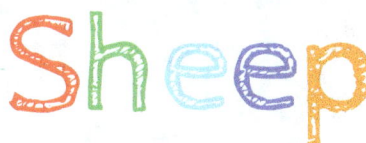

④

⑤

⑥

Sheep

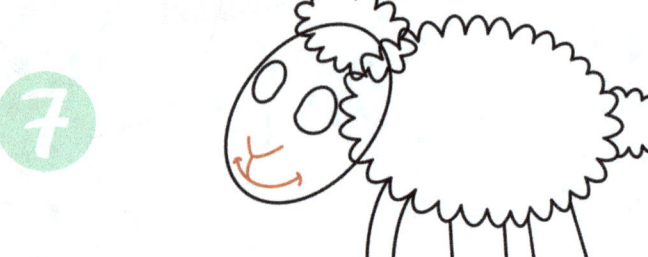

7

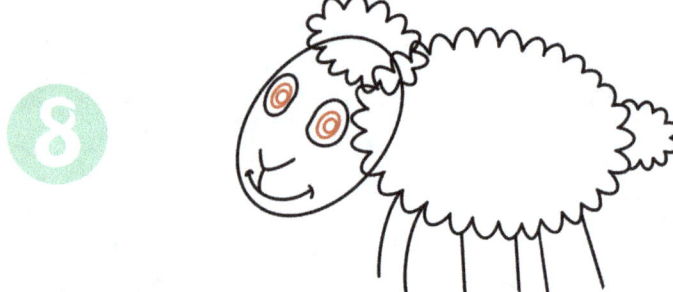

8

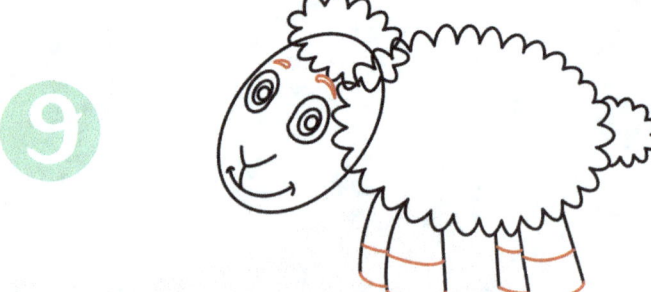

9

Sheep

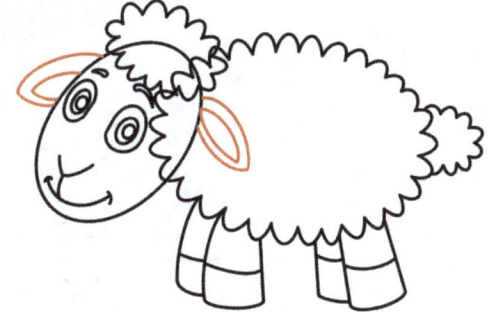

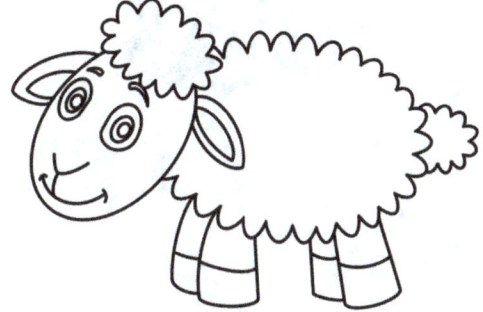

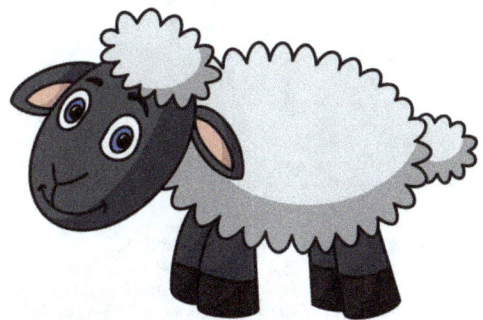

Sheep

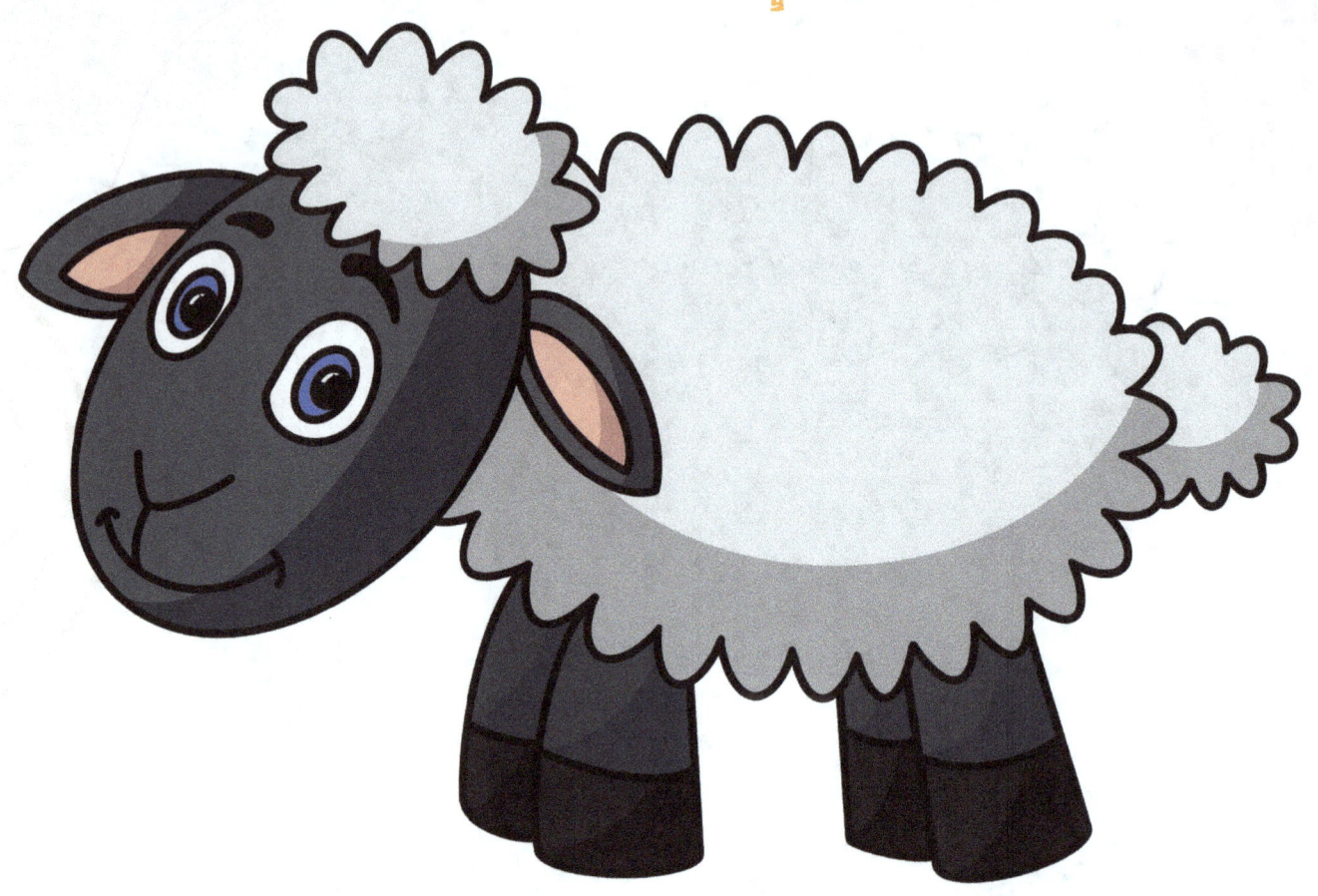

Horse

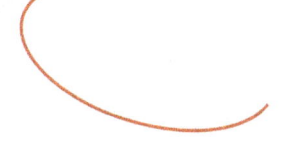

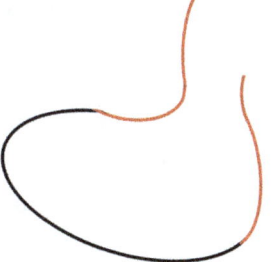

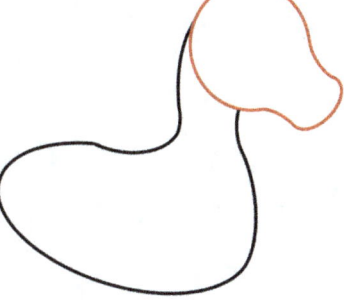

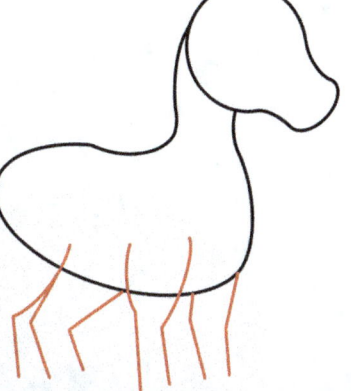

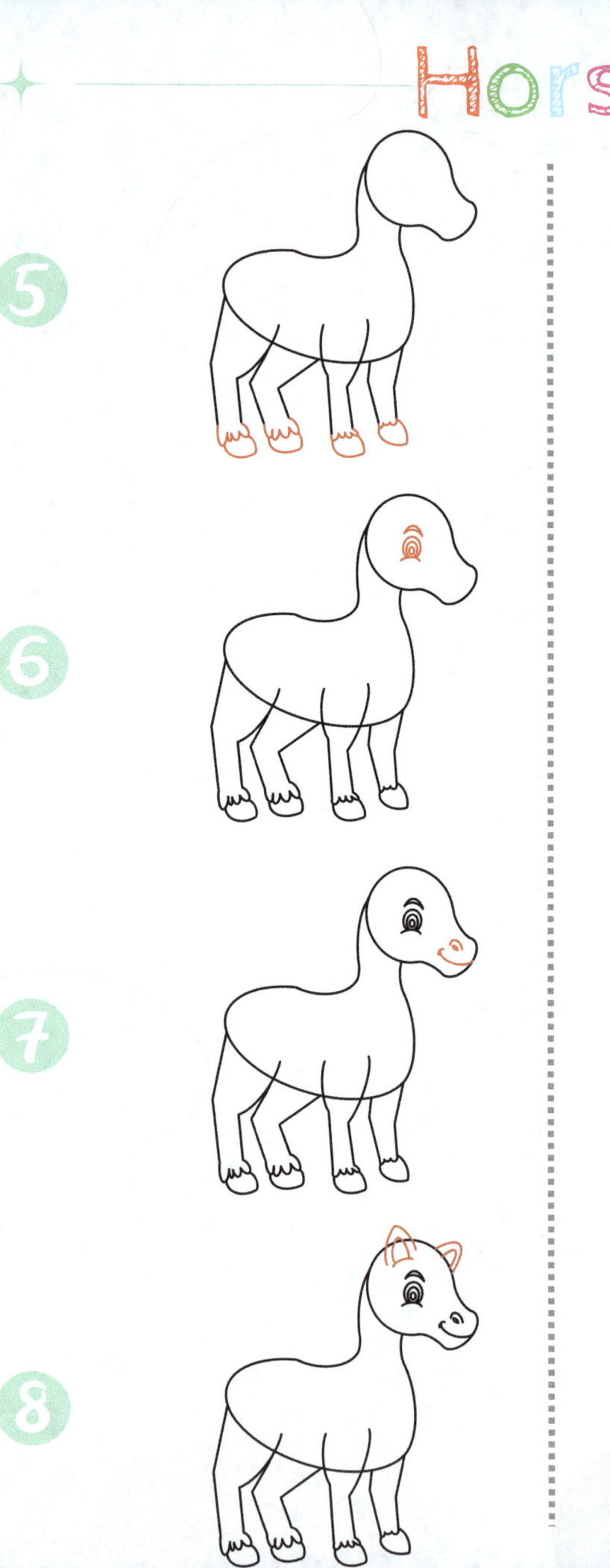

Horse

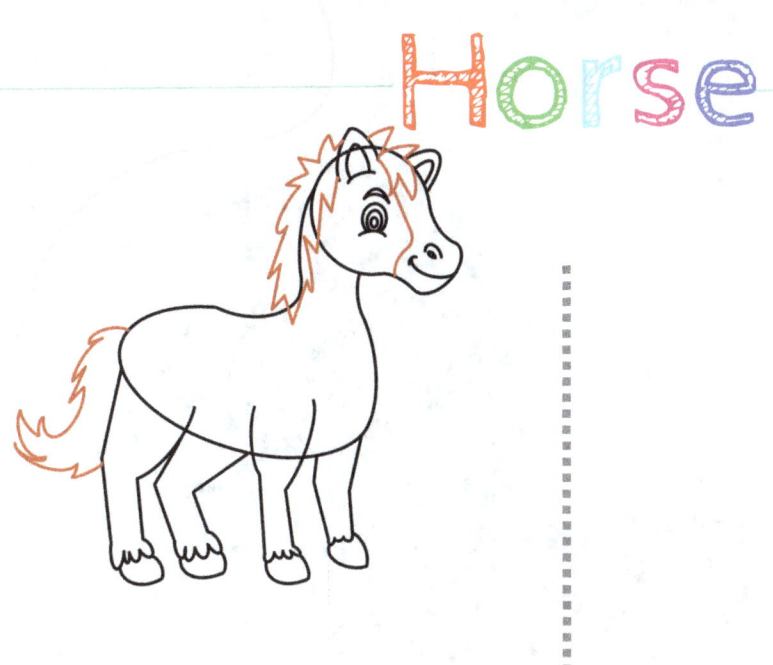

9

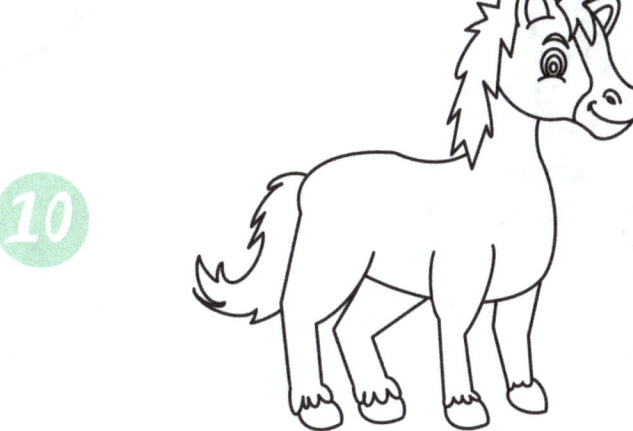

10

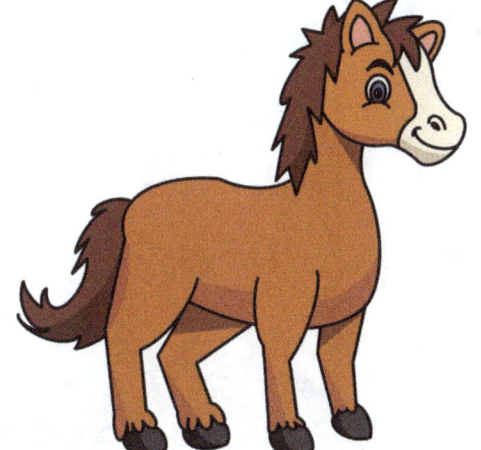

11

Horse

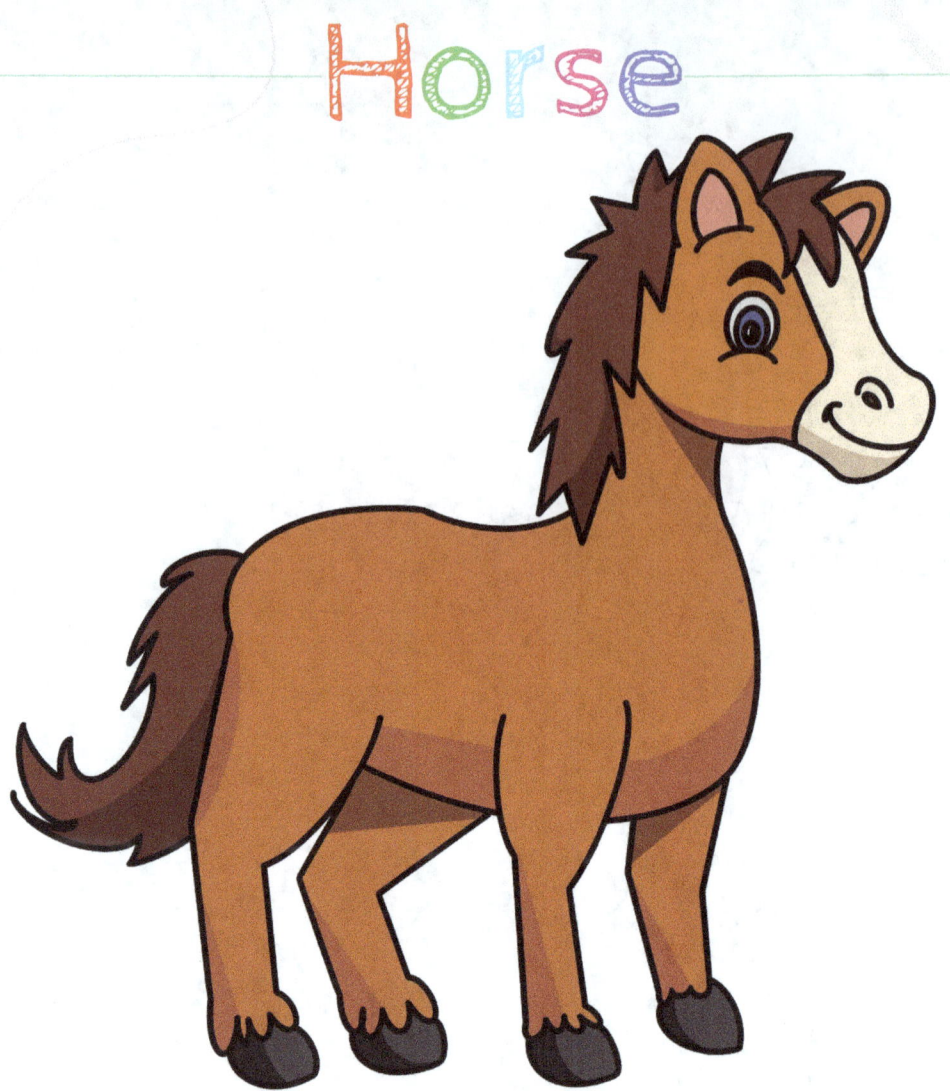

Kangaroo

1

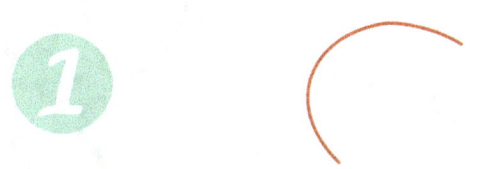

2

3

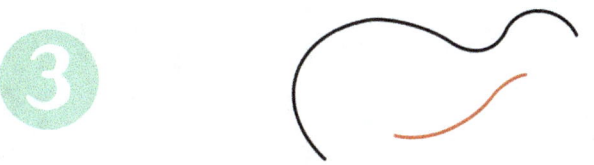

Kangaroo

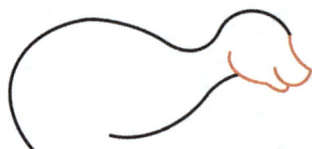

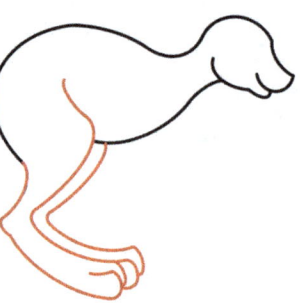

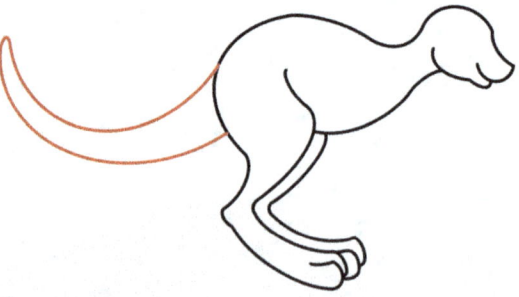

Kangaroo

7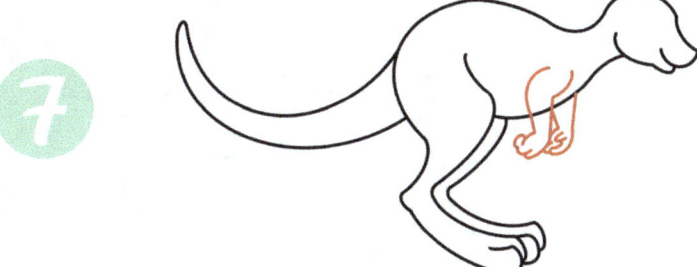

8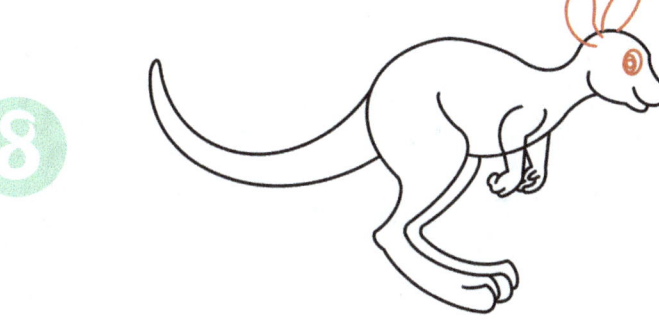

9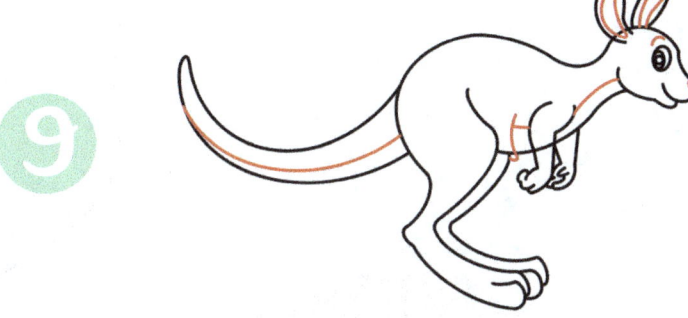

Kangaroo

10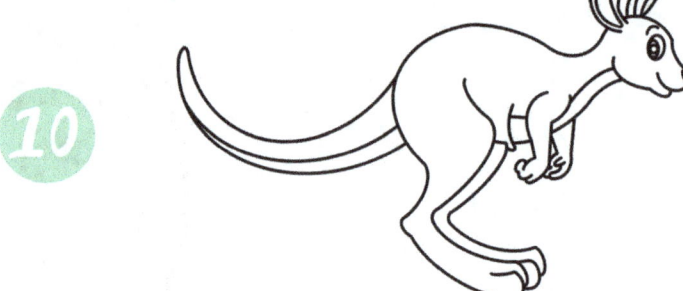

11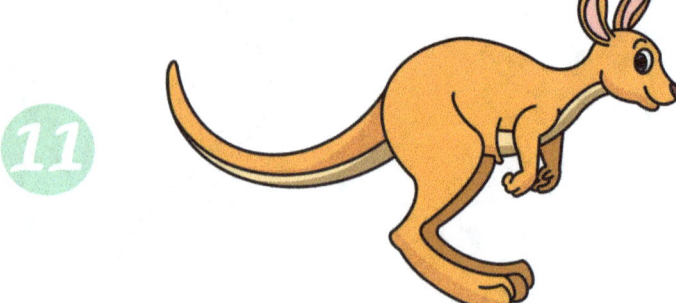

Kangaroo

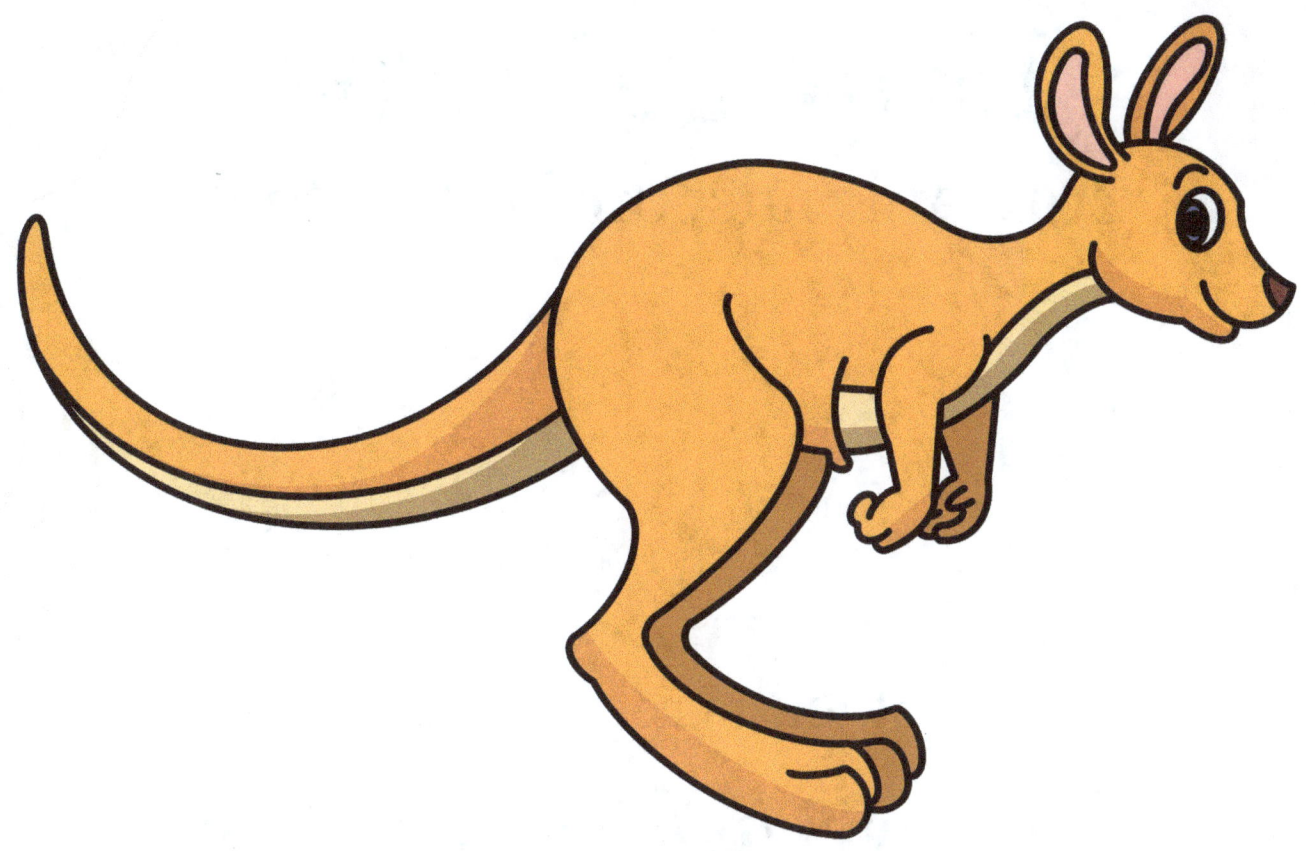

Kangaroo

How to Draw

Cute animals, birds & insects

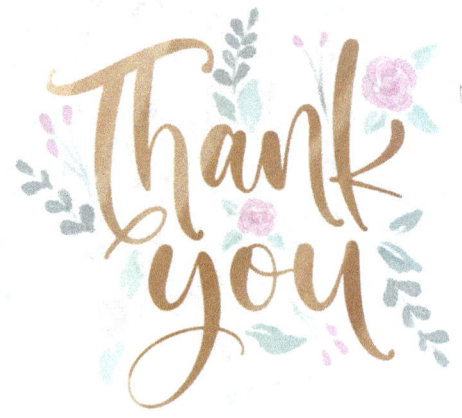

Please contact us regarding any queries:

 **joyblendarts@gmail.com**

We also make custom/personalized books

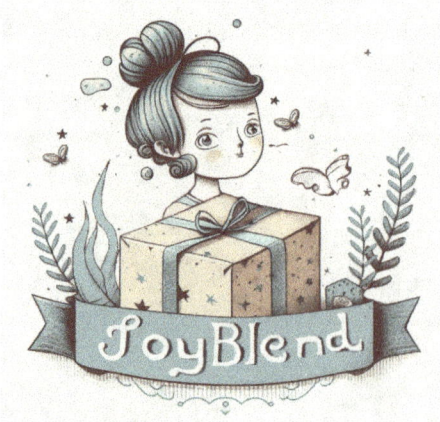

Only for personal use.